BAUHAUS
DESSAU
ARCHITECTURE

BAUHAUS DESSAU ARCHITECTURE

FLORIAN STROB
THOMAS MEYER

Bauhaus Dessau
Foundation

HIRMER

Kornhaus Restaurant

New Masters' Houses

Masters' Houses

Bauhaus Building

Engemann House
and the group of houses on
Fischererweg/Stephanweg

Naurath and
Hahn Houses

Employment
Office

Dessau-Törten Housing Estate

Fieger House
Steel House

Paulick
Row Houses

Houses with
Balcony Access

CONTENTS

FOREWORD

To mark the centenary of the founding of the Bauhaus, the Bauhaus Dessau Foundation is newly presenting the Dessau Bauhaus buildings, the greatest and most important treasures of its collection, in this publication. The photographs by Thomas Meyer show a wide range of Bauhaus architecture – from the Kornhaus Restaurant on the River Elbe in the north to the Dessau-Törten Housing Estate with the Konsum Building and the Houses with Balcony Access by Hannes Meyer – in their present state, revealing a lot about the history, use, impact, appropriation and atmosphere of these icons of classical modernism. Both the properties owned by the Bauhaus Dessau Foundation and the publicly and privately owned buildings built by Bauhaus architects between 1925 and 1932 are covered.

As witnesses of that period, the Dessau Bauhaus buildings not only give visitors and the readers of this book an understanding of the historical Bauhaus, but to this day also bear the marks of time and its vicissitudes. Rather than keeping these marks hidden and secret, they should be incorporated into the narrative as evidence of events. For this reason, the photographs of Thomas Meyer show not only the architecture that is preserved in the original, or reconstructed based on the original, but also the signs of use over the decades. In his texts, Florian Strob explains the innovations and intentions of the architects, while at the same time discussing the reception and the modifications of the Dessau Bauhaus buildings.

Starting in the spring of 2019, the Bauhaus Dessau Foundation will, for the first time, curate the Dessau Bauhaus buildings with an overarching concept. Moreover, the new Bauhaus Museum Dessau will join the urban landscape of the historical Bauhaus buildings in September 2019, when it will be inaugurated as a venue for changing exhibitions with the presentation of its collection. The museum is conceived as an open stage which carries into the city – in much the same way that the Dessau Bauhaus buildings were never mere sites of museumisation, but were, and are, constantly transformed by their use and updated. Even to the Bauhaus architects, their work was never an artistic end in itself; instead, the basis for their practice was, as Walter Gropius wrote in 1930 in the foreword to his publication *bauhausbauten dessau*, the "social idea of the unity of all creative work in its relationship to life itself".

Claudia Perren
Director and CEO of the Bauhaus Dessau Foundation

Today, the hall for construction theory is often used for seminars, and chairs and tables have been newly acquired for this purpose. The lights were designed by Marianne Brandt. The windowsills are so deep that they were used as a storage area for drawings, and wooden bars had to be attached to open the windows.

THE DESSAU BAUHAUS BUILDINGS TODAY

The Swiss writer Peter Bichsel once remarked in conversation that something is modern when it surprises him. And modernism, he added, means that a work is not to be taken for granted. In 2019, the Bauhaus celebrates the centenary of its founding. Perhaps one of the best-known schools of modernism, it has indeed been universally talked about – hailed and cursed, reinvented and critically relativised – over the past one hundred years. As a result, the Bauhaus has become a natural part of history and, consequently, of our present as well.

The tendency to take the Bauhaus for granted is especially true of the buildings the Bauhaus realised in Dessau: from the Bauhaus Building and the Masters' Houses to the Dessau-Törten Housing Estate. In the 1920s and early 1930s, the Bauhaus and the Bauhäusler themselves had, through the prolific publication of photographs, footage and texts, significantly contributed to turning the completed buildings into icons of modern architecture.

The aim of this book, therefore, is to not take for granted the "Bauhausbauten Dessau", which is how founding director Walter Gropius referred to them as early as 1930 in the title of his book, and instead to take a productive step back from them in order to show them in their complexity. With this publication, we wish to free the Bauhaus as Neues Bauen (New Building) – to which the element of the new was, by its very programme, of particular importance – from the shock-induced paralysis of the all too familiar.

For this to succeed, this book covers not only the buildings which Gropius counted among the Dessau Bauhaus buildings: Gropius included in his canon only those buildings in which his own architecture office had been involved and which, to this day, define the public perception of Dessau Bauhaus architecture. There are, however, other buildings aside from the Bauhaus Building and the Masters' Houses, such as the Kornhaus Restaurant by Carl Fieger and the conservatively modernist middle-class residences by Friedrich Engemann – both Fieger and Engemann taught at the Dessau Bauhaus and therefore the buildings they built locally also rank among the Bauhaus buildings. At the same time, the careful objectivity of the brilliant new photographs

Carl Fieger, the Fieger House in Dessau-Törten, 1927, photographer unknown, Bauhaus Dessau Foundation, inv. I 20290 F

by Thomas Meyer paint the most comprehensive picture possible of the architecture. From the outset, it was our plan not to monumentalise or musealise the buildings, not to depict them as chic empty shells (which they were never intended to be), and thus to avoid blocking out certain essential aspects.

This approach also means that the uses, along with the alterations and renovations, are just as much part of the narrative and that Bauhaus architecture did not have only Marcel Breuer's famous cantilever chairs standing it. In the row houses of the Dessau-Törten Housing Estate, for instance, a composting toilet in the stable also reveals something important about the buildings. The row houses designed by the architect Richard Paulick, on the other hand, were given pitched roofs for ideological reasons during the National Socialist era; their renovation in the 1990s left them unrecognisable, from the outside, as Bauhaus buildings. Or take the private residence of the architect Carl Fieger: not only was it modified and considerably enlarged by an addition, but it now also stands in an enchanted, overgrown garden, which considerably obstructs the view of the building, especially during the summer months. When we compare this rampant vegetation with the originally austere, plain and functional gardens of the Bauhaus buildings, then that too is – without judging the current state – perhaps another surprising change.

A further issue is that we can document only one temporary state of renovation of the buildings. In the course of each renovation, new insights regarding the original building and its state at the time of its completion are gained and implemented. An impressive example of this is the workshop wing of the Bauhaus Building with its world-famous glass curtain wall, which was destroyed by a bomb hit during World War II and then, in various extensive renovations over the course of decades, recreated ever more closely to the original. Extensive research and renovation work on the buildings was carried out again as part of the 2019 Bauhaus anniversary. Temporarily installed frames for renovation can be seen, for instance, in front of the windows in the semicircular Kopfbau, or head-end structure, of the historical Employment Office (even though it was not until years after completion of the building that windows were inserted into the structure); the colour scheme of the walls in the Houses with Balcony Access, as documented in this volume, has in the meantime been reworked. The wall colours of the Kandinsky and Klee Masters' Houses now glow even more brightly; and on the Konsum Building, we will soon see the lettering "Konsumverein für Dessau und Umgegend E.G.M.B.H" again.

This publication aims to offer readers a hopefully instructive mix of recognisables and surprises, and it does this based on the clear belief that any relevance of the past can only be assigned to it by the present. And with this focused view from the present to the past, the Bauhaus buildings in Dessau may perhaps surprise us again – just as they surprised people back in the Bauhaus days, when the buildings were anything but taken for granted.

Richard Paulick, row houses, balconies on the south façade, c.1930

The Dessau Bauhaus Building, view of the workshop wing from the north-east, state in July 1953, photographer unknown, Bauhaus Dessau Foundation, inv. I 17150 F

BAUHAUS AND MODERNISM

The Bauhaus (1919–33) was a school which combined art, crafts and technology in a radically new way. In Dessau between 1925 and 1932, the already world-renowned Bauhaus tested the city of tomorrow. What the Bauhaus built and lived there had a model character. The Bauhäusler created prototypes of modernism and realised new forms of social coexistence.

The Bauhaus aimed at nothing less than changing and improving the living conditions of people through modern design. The various arts, technology and, in the early years of the school, especially the crafts were to contribute collaboratively to construction in order to meet this goal. Not until its move to Dessau in 1925 was the Bauhaus able to subject its ideas to a reality test. Only here did it become possible – if we leave the Sommerfeld House in Berlin (1922) and the experimental 1923 Haus Am Horn in Weimar aside – to actually build. The city is also the only location of the school where all three directors, Walter Gropius (1919–28), Hannes Meyer (1928–30) and Ludwig Mies van der Rohe (1930–33), were active.

For the Bauhaus, Dessau thus became a kind of rehearsal stage for a new world. The school's directors and professors tended to realise the buildings through their own architecture offices, yet the Bauhaus workshops and the students were often also involved. This aspect took on particular importance during the tenure of Hannes Meyer, the second director, for according to his pedagogical concept, teaching was to be linked even more closely to architectural practice.

In retrospect, the city of Dessau today also appears to be a kind of rehearsal stage because the Bauhäusler tested solutions there for a variety of building tasks: from mansions and row houses to the apartment building, from the school building and the restaurant to the employment office. However, it is often overlooked that these buildings were not the only ones on this stage. The Bauhaus was part of the New Building school in Dessau and Germany and, beyond that, part of international modernism. "New Building" generally refers to a movement in architecture and urban planning in the first quarter of the twentieth century which tackled the existing housing shortage through economical construction and design. Social aspects were especially important in this context: most of the housing estates and other buildings with functional geometric layouts were realised in municipalities with social democratic governments. It therefore makes no sense to speak of a "Bauhaus style", as there was often no significant stylistic difference between works by Bauhaus architects and those of other protagonists of New Building in Germany.

As a school, the Bauhaus may be considered a crucial node in the network of modernism, but when reading this book we should not forget that it is worth exploring the immediate and wider context of the buildings and that what is presented here in pictures and words is just a small and very particular segment of modern architecture. Let us take the example of the architect Leopold Fischer, who as a student of Adolf Loos and with his own buildings – for instance, for the Anhaltische Siedlerverband (an Anhaltinian housing association) in Dessau and environs – can obviously be categorised as modernist. Both his competition as a housing planner in Dessau (after a brief collaboration in the architecural office of Walter Gropius) and his refusal to run the Bauhaus Building Department put Fischer at a conscious distance from the Bauhaus. For this reason, his works have not been considered in the context of this volume.

This publication includes only those buildings which were realised by Bauhäusler, or with their involvement, between 1925 and 1932, when the school was operating in Dessau. This definition covers works by the three aforementioned directors, Gropius, Meyer and Mies van der Rohe, as well as by the architects Carl Fieger and Richard Paulick, both of whom worked for a while in the architecture office of Walter Gropius and were in close dialogue with the Bauhaus; from 1927 on, Fieger also taught as an adjunct in the Building Department of the Bauhaus. The residential houses of the architect and occasional deputy director Friedrich Engemann are also among the Bauhaus buildings understood in this way, even if their more moderate or conservative modernism does not, at first glance, fit the general picture of the Bauhaus. The Steel House, as a joint project of Richard Paulick and the painter and Bauhaus master Georg Muche, who had already designed the Haus Am Horn (1923) in Weimar, is likewise part of this book.

During World War II, two of the Masters' Houses were destroyed; the garden wall of the director's mansion and, as part of that wall, the Trinkhalle (kiosk) – Mies van der Rohe's only building in Dessau – were mostly torn down during GDR times. In 2014, the repair of the ensemble of Masters' Houses was completed: for the so-called New Masters' Houses, including the Trinkhalle, the clients in coordination with ICOMOS decided against reconstruction in favour of a more abstract engagement with the legacy of the Bauhaus, which was then reflected in the concept of the architectural office of Bruno Fioretti Marquez. This contemporary approach to the (lost) Bauhaus buildings invites us to take another, fresh and different look at the historical buildings and their history. In this sense, we gladly included in this volume the New Masters' Houses as part of the historical ensemble.

Instead of organising the Bauhaus buildings in Dessau by architects or by year of completion, they have been geographically divided into three chapters: in the north of Dessau, the Bauhaus Building with the Masters' Houses, the residential houses by Paulick and Engemann, as well as the Kornhaus on the banks of the River Elbe; in the centre of the city, the Employment Office; and finally, in the south, the Dessau-Törten Housing Estate with its different stages and special buildings. Each of these chapters begins with a map section, each building is presented in texts and photographs, and ground floor plans are added for better understanding.

Dessau, January 2019

Leopold Fischer, semi-detached houses on Großring in Dessau, view in 1930, photo from *Die Heimat*, supplement of the *Anhalter Anzeiger*, 5 April 1930

Kornhaus Restaurant

New Masters' Houses

Masters' Houses

Bauhaus Building

Engemann House
and the group of houses on
Fischereiweg/Stephanweg

Naurath and
Hahn Houses

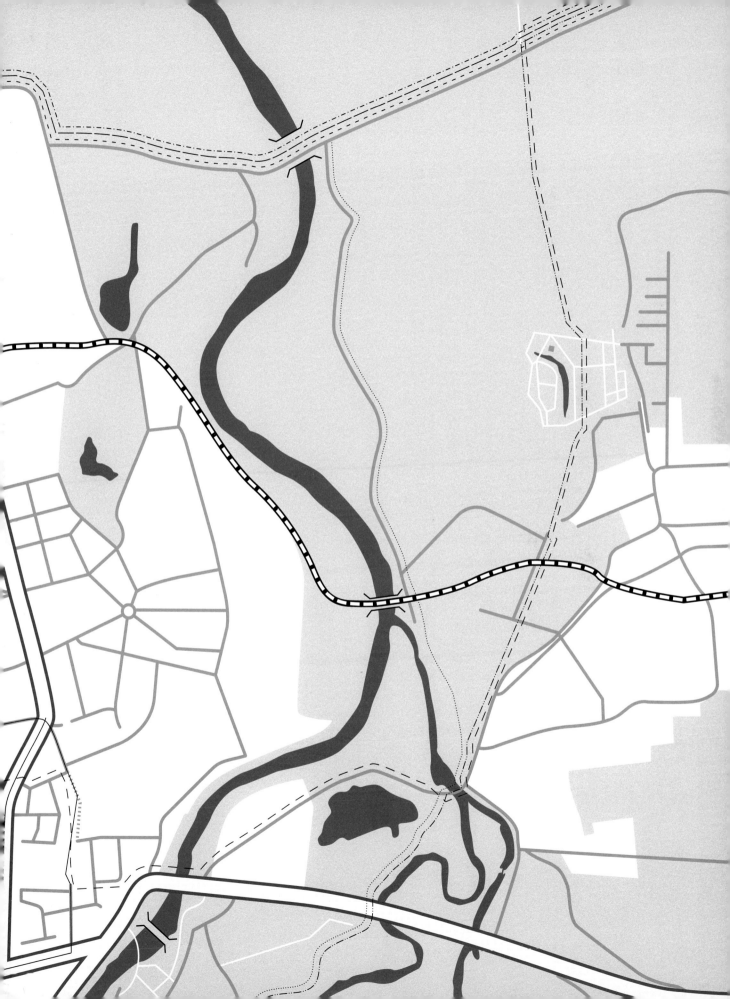

BAUHAUS BUILDING

WALTER GROPIUS
1925/26

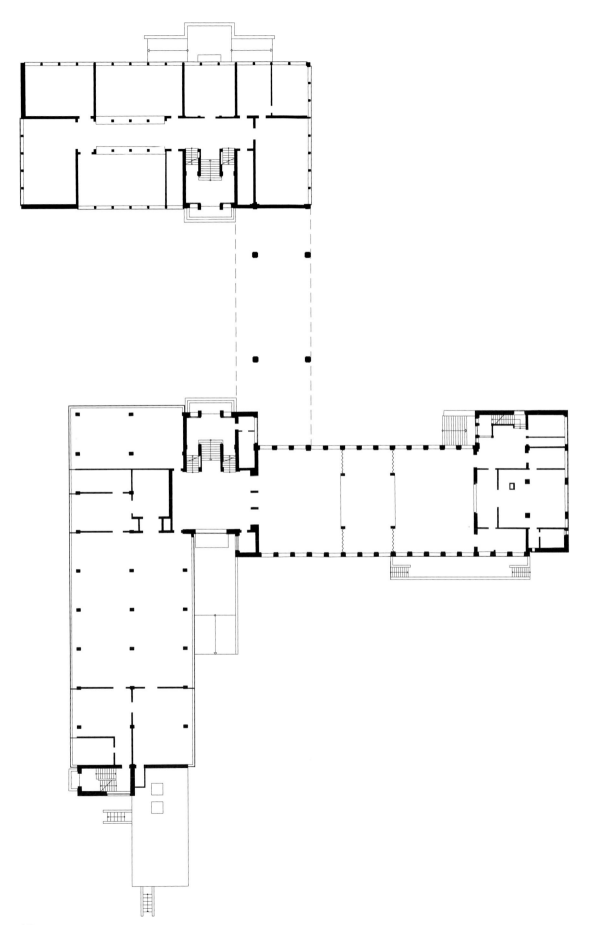

Ground floor

The Bauhaus school building in Dessau is one of the best-known and most significant buildings of twentieth-century architecture. Few other buildings of the past century have been depicted as often, discussed as much and received this degree of global attention. Any student of architecture, no matter where in the world, has come across it – and not just once. Whether it is seen as a successful or unsuccessful design is hardly relevant: the Bauhaus Building is part of the canon of world architecture.

THE BAUHAUS IN DESSAU: 1925–32

When the Bauhaus moved from Weimar to Dessau in the spring of 1925, Walter Gropius, the school's first director, was given the opportunity to create a school building and a housing complex for the Bauhaus masters. The site for the construction of the school was located in the city expansion area north-west of the train station. When, after more than a year in temporary Dessau accommodations, the Bauhaus Building was ready to be inaugurated and moved into on 4 December 1926, it stood like a glassy and white-plastered exclamation mark of modernism in an area that was still largely unbuilt at the time. With the upper structure deliberately overhanging a dark-painted souterrain, it seemed almost to be hovering.

The design by Gropius's architecture office assembled various functions into a building. It dispensed with the symmetry of a single structure that was expected at the time; instead, each function received its own building which, while being interconnected with the others, remains legible as a distinct structure. The first impression this design concept evokes in the viewer is that of movement: you have to walk around and tour the building to grasp it in its entirety, as no two sections are alike.

When Gropius was given the opportunity to create a school building for the Bauhaus, one condition imposed by the city of Dessau was that the municipal technical school should also receive a new building nearby. Conveniently, a street – the Leopolddank, today Bauhausstrasse – cut through the site, and Gropius decided to locate the Technische Lehranstalten (technical schools) north of the street and the Bauhaus south of it. Both are connected via an elevated administrative wing called the *Brücke*, or bridge.

Instead of the Technische Lehranstalten, the Gewerbliche Berufsschule (vocational technical school) moved into the north part of the building when it was completed. Even though their buildings were connected, cooperation between the two schools proved difficult. A few teachers of the Gewerbliche Berufsschule were hired as adjuncts to teach specialised classes at the Bauhaus, but beyond this the relationship was a rather sceptical one. Perhaps the differences between a conservative vocational school and the experimental Bauhaus were too great.

While the part located north of the street accommodated the vocational school in a single structure by dint of ribbon windows and equal-size classrooms, the connected Bauhaus to the south of it was divided into various structures: the workshop wing with the world-famous and at the time revolutionary, industrial-looking glass curtain wall; the large stairwell as a vertical connecting element between the workshop and the administrative wings and a place of communication; the horizontal *Festebene*, or festive area, with exhibition space, vestibule, auditorium, stage and canteen, which, as the social hub of the Bauhaus, extends from the workshop wing to the studio building. Finally, rising in the east, the studio building offering studio space for twenty-eight students and featuring its famous balconies and a roof terrace for gymnastics.

Just listing these individual parts already illustrates what Walter Gropius achieved here in a programmatic manner: the combination of teaching, work, festiveness and life in one building. Today, one would probably speak of a "campus", which is derived from the Latin for "field". Since the eighteenth century, this term has been used in the USA to describe university facilities. There, the buildings for teaching and the accommodations for professors and students were usually built outside the city in a park-like setting, a "field" of sorts. The Bauhaus, however, was not just a campus outside the city gates, in an area that was still largely unbuilt at the time; it also offered a view north across the field to the Georgium, which is part of the Dessau-Wörlitz Garden Realm. In spatial terms, this park from the late eighteenth century related the Bauhaus to the Enlightenment, which in Dessau found its architectural expression above all in the English landscape garden and its buildings.

To the west and south of the Bauhaus, visitors today can still find clues as to why Dessau was chosen as the new site for the Bauhaus in 1925: located there are, among others, the Hugo Junkers Technical Museum and the adjacent Dessau airfield. Both places typify the emerging industrial city at the beginning of the twentieth century. Approaching the Bauhaus from the south in 1926, on the present-day Gropiusallee, one headed from the modern industrial area towards the Georgium and passed the Bauhaus Building with its famous lettering along the way. Thus, even the organisation of urban space is illustrative of Gropius's motto for the Bauhaus: "Art and Technology – A New Unity".

The same aspiration also finds expression in many places inside the building. In the Bauhaus stairwell, for instance, on the landing between the vestibule and the first floor, a radiator is installed above two doors – deliberately so, for while this is not an ideal location for heating purposes, it was where paintings would have been hung in the imposing main stairwell of older buildings. Gropius put the radiator in the place of the picture, technology in the place of art.

Technology is displayed wherever technology would have been depicted in a painting. Work itself is shown wherever work would have been shown in a picture. When entering the Bauhaus Building through the main entrance, visitors climb a few steps to the vestibule and are drawn in by the light that enters through a huge glass pane – at the time an expensive, technically challenging solution for a window. Visitors standing in the elaborately designed vestibule look out through this pane of glass at the fully glazed workshop wing. Instead of presenting a mural on the subject of work and industriousness, Gropius showed the architecture itself and the students as workers at the Bauhaus.

At the same time, this illustrates something that visitors first experience here and which then recurs throughout the tour of the building: they keep looking *out of* the building *at* the building. The configuration of the whole is clearly revealed to the viewer, and the building becomes a perception machine. This includes the use of glass as a construction material, whose transparency allows visitors to look through it, only to deny them that possibility a moment later with its reflections.

Besides offering an impressive view of the workshop wing with its glass-and-steel curtain wall, the vestibule itself was also very specifically designed: the lacquer surfaces of the three doors to the auditorium, the tubular lamps and the terrazzo flooring attract the visitors' attention. Everything here appears exquisite, almost dignified. Throughout the building – for all its perceived simplicity or plainness at first glance – it is recommended to pay attention to the materials and colours. Several Bauhäusler, masters and students alike, contributed to the interior decoration. László Moholy-Nagy was responsible for the colour design of the vestibule; the tubular lamps were the work of Max Krajewski, a student; the globe lights found in many places in the building were by Marianne Brandt; and Marcel Breuer designed the tubular steel seating of the auditorium and also tables and stools in the canteen.

The colour scheme by Hinnerk Scheper is particularly important for the overall appearance of the Bauhaus. Rhythms that are often a result of the construction and found throughout the building (such as the striking beams in the hallway of the north wing) are further accentuated by Scheper's colour scheme. Movement is thus evident on the outside in the individual joined structures, yet the interior, too, has a certain dynamic of its own. "White" modernism was in reality colourful and through-composed like a piece of music. It was most certainly a far cry from the monotony nowadays associated with the notion of functionalism.

Functionalism at the Bauhaus is not synonymous with a complete lack of sensuality, as indicated by the ingenious use of materials throughout the building, which appeals to all the senses. One would almost want to plead with visitors before they enter to use not just their sense of vision, but also to hear, smell and feel. The banging of the doors and the subsequent echos can be heard everywhere. When closing a door, the door leaf is to be pushed very gently against the frame. Yet even then, the closing is still clearly audible at a distance. The cushioning rubber is missing.

The original Triolin flooring in the director's office is largely preserved. The door to this room is rarely open; in this way, the strong, distinctly sweetish smell of the Triolin remains in the room and surprises anyone who enters. The synthetic material was developed in Germany in the 1920s as a cheaper substitute for the more expensive linoleum. In general, the floors at the Bauhaus would merit a separate chapter. Depending on the function of the spaces, different flooring was chosen, with the quality of the materials also revealing something significant about the character of the particular space. When we compare, say, the terrazzo in the ground-floor vestibule with the xylolite screed in the areas in front of the workshops, we find that the flooring itself already points to the functions of the spaces as "festive reception" and "functional work".

The configuration of the bridge on the first floor was particularly impressive through the transition of the flooring. The generously glazed entrance to the space causes one to first look to the side, before the flooring changes: from cold to warm, from the grey beige of the xylolite screed to the red of the linoleum used today (the original flooring was probably Triolin, but this cannot be proven with certainty). One's full attention is then drawn to the incredibly long ribbon window uninterrupted by pillars, which Hinnerk Scheper further accentuated with a stripe of red paint underneath and above the windows in the centre. Like so much else in and about this building, nothing like that had ever been seen before in 1926. It was a bold start into architectural modernism.

THE BAUHAUS BUILDING AFTER THE BAUHAUS

This programmatically posited and emphatically asserted boldness of modernism was undoubtedly also what made the National Socialists deem it necessary to put a slightly pitched gable roof on the Bauhaus Building. The Bauhaus logo was removed and the swastika flag was hoisted on the studio building. The Nazi Party pushed through the closure of the Bauhaus by 30 September 1932. On 1 October, Nazi stormtroopers and auxiliary police forces burnt all the writings left behind by Ludwig Mies van der Rohe, the last director of the Bauhaus. The Landesfrauenarbeitsschule (Federal School for Women Workers) moved in, with some rooms also being occupied by the Gauamtswalterschule (school for Gau officials) of the Nazi Party and Albert Speer's Building Staff. Later, the building was used for a while by the Wehrmacht and the Junkers aircraft and engine works.

In 1945, the city of Dessau was bombed by allied forces and more than eighty per cent of its building stock was destroyed. The Bauhaus Building, although listed as a building worthy of preservation, was also affected. Bombs hit the workshop and north wings; the building was partly gutted by fire and lost its eye-catching glass façade and the white plaster. Yet the load-bearing structure of reinforced concrete, stone-iron ceilings and brick wall fillings was preserved, so that after some repair work the building could be used again. However, the Bauhaus Building had lost is glass façade for decades to come; brickwork and small windows were used in its place.

In the GDR, the Bauhaus Building continued to serve as a school, housing the vocational schools of the city of Dessau until 1988. A first restoration was undertaken in 1965, and in 1976 a second restoration was completed, which also involved restoring the curtain wall of the workshop wing. At the same time, the Wissenschaftlich-Kulturelle Zentrum (Academic Cultural Centre) was founded, followed in 1994 by the establishment of the Bauhaus Dessau Foundation.

Today, the Bauhaus Building in Dessau, which was named a UNESCO World Heritage site in 1996, is once again a place where people pursuing different activities and interests converge, just as they did in the period from 1926 until 1932. On the one hand, selected rooms are available for visitors to learn more about the Bauhaus, its architecture, teaching, faculty and students. On the other hand, the building houses the Stiftung Bauhaus Dessau, which organises artistic and scholarly programmes to educate about the ideas and issues of the Bauhaus and keep them alive in our present day. The former student studios are even available for overnight lodging.

Today, most visitors come from the direction of the train station and first see the studio building (seen on the right). In 1926, people usually approached the "school of design" from the south – which is why the famous lettering was placed here.

In 1926, people would come from the south and first pass by the glass curtain wall of the workshop wing, and then turn right to get to the school's main entrance. A part of the basement level bumps out on the south side of the workshop wing. On the left is a surviving door handle.

Even in 1926, visitors already entered the building
through the red doors and were then greeted by wide
stairs leading up to the light-filled vestibule. The symmetry
of this impressive reception contrasts with the asymmetry
of the overall complex.

Elaborate terrazzo flooring adorns the vestibule, and the tubular lamps by Bauhaus student Max Krajewski point to the doors of the auditorium. In the stairwell, industrial technology, such as the window opening mechanism and the boldly placed radiator, meets the building's rich colour scheme.

On the different levels of the workshop wing, the students acquired craft skills in bright daylight. The famous glass curtain wall was destroyed in World War II and reconstructed only decades later. Rather than the original steel, aluminium was used for the new curtain wall.

As the former administrative wing, the so-called bridge connects the Bauhaus in the south to the Technische Lehranstalten (technical schools) in the north. Also located on the bridge was the office of Bauhaus director Walter Gropius. Its colour scheme and furnishings were reconstructed based on the current state of research.

The north wing housed the Technische Lehranstalten (technical schools). While this part of the building was less transparent in terms of its design than the workshop wing, Hinnerk Scheper's colour scheme continues here in hues that are all the bolder. The door signs, door handles and fire extinguishers are not original.

The stairwell in the north wing is located across from
the south stairwell. The materials and configuration are
the same, but the colour and light produce different
impressions of the spaces. The hand rails are original,
the lamp is by Marianne Brandt.

The tables and stools in the canteen were designed by Marcel Breuer, but these are true-to-the-original replicas. Today, visitors can have lunch in the canteen (top). Behind the sliding wall is the stage, which continues to be used for performances and concerts.

A view from the stage into the auditorium with its characteristic tubular steel seating by Marcel Breuer (reconstruction). The boards of the stage are still the original ones. During the most recent renovation, they were installed upside down to preserve the original material as long as possible.

The stairwell of the studio building (left) also features a
colour scheme. The rooms were merged into classrooms
under the third Bauhaus director, Ludwig Mies van der
Rohe. Historical photographs were used in the
reconstruction of some of the rooms.

The studio building was (and still is) a popular subject for photos. Today, it houses students and visitors may rent rooms for overnight accommodation.

MASTERS' HOUSES

WALTER GROPIUS
1925/26

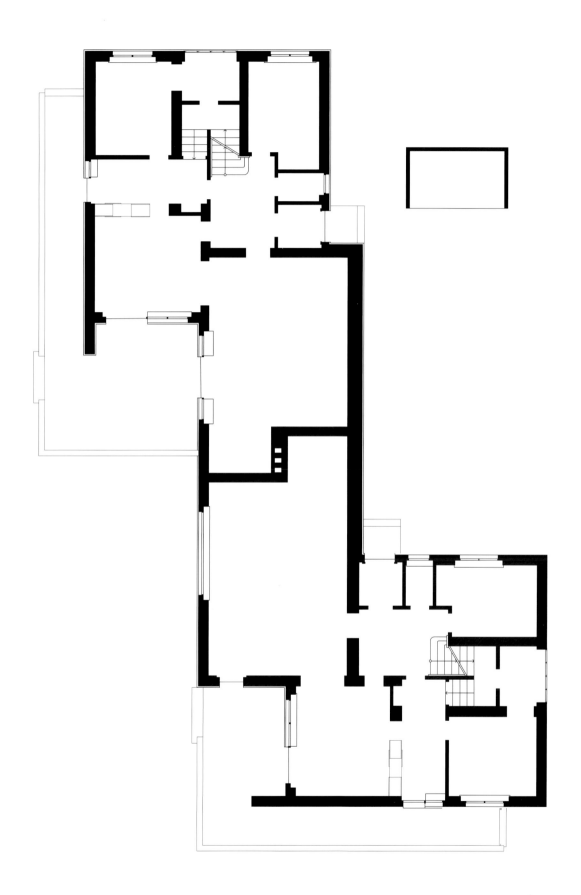

Ground floor
of a Master's House

The Masters' Houses near the Bauhaus Building in Dessau are among the seminal prototypes for modern living in Germany. In designing the Dessau model housing estate, Walter Gropius and the Bauhaus looked for ways to organise modern living in contemporary fashion. Between 1926 and 1932, the housing estate was at the same time perhaps the best-known artist colony of the Weimar Republic, with such famous residents as Wassily Kandinsky, Paul Klee and Oskar Schlemmer.

THE MASTERS' HOUSES: 1925–32

When the Bauhaus moved to Dessau in 1925, Walter Gropius was commissioned by the city to not only realise a school building, but also to build residences and studio buildings for six Bauhaus masters and for himself as the school's director. During a walk with then Dessau mayor Fritz Hesse, Mr. and Mrs. Gropius chose a lot lined with pines on Burgkühnauer Allee, today Ebertallee, for this purpose.

The area is located between two grounds of the Dessau-Wörlitzer Garden Realm, an English landscape garden from the eighteenth century. At one end of the tree-lined street are the Seven Pillars, a scaled-down copy of the classical Temple of Saturn in Rome, and at the other end is the Amaliensitz, a classicist structure by Friedrich Wilhelm von Erdmannsdorff. It was into this cultural landscape of the Enlightenment that Gropius placed his design for the director's residence and the three pairs of semi-detached houses for the Bauhaus masters.

The design was developed at the architecture office of Walter Gropius in collaboration with Carl Fieger, Ernst Neufert and others. The white-plastered, markedly horizontal cubes of the houses still offer an appealing contrast to the dark, vertical pine trunks surrounding them. The large cantilevered balconies, moreover, create the impression that the cubes are hovering between the trees. The long, vertical windows of the stairwells, which take up the verticality of the pine trees, create tension in the sculptural composition of the houses.

The ensemble of buildings was planned according to the principle of "large-scale building blocks". Gropius had first developed this idea in the early 1920s. For individual functions, he designed individual structures which were to be produced ahead as variable set pieces like building blocks and could then be put together depending on the building project. In this way, Gropius aimed to realise the principles of rational building both in the design of architecture and in the actual construction process.

It was not uncommon for such ideas for standardisation to be developed in response to the housing shortage after World War I. Yet for all the standardisation, Gropius's design for the Masters' Houses aspired to avoid monotony. Instead, the motto was "Variety through Standardisation". By mirroring and rotating the floor plans of the semi-detached houses, Gropius managed to realise this principle most impressively in the Dessau Masters' Houses. To this day, the Masters' Houses demonstrate the spatial possibilities of the building-block or modular approach to design, though the actual construction process did not yet meet the standards of prefabrication and was instead still marked by craftsmanship.

Though created in the context of the housing shortage after World War I, they are nonetheless housing for middle-class living and artistic work. The aim was to create the modern artist's residence as a cross between country house and mansion.

A TOUR OF THE HOUSE

Visitors approach the Masters' Houses along a straight footpath leading through a wide, public front garden. The white cubes on the large, park-like site are elegantly set back from the street. The design of the front garden is extremely reduced: pines, short grass and dark, low metal rods enclosing it. The footpath runs past bicycle garages towards the front door of the semi-detached house on the right, then makes a ninety-degree turn to the left and runs underneath the large side-by-side first-floor windows of the adjacent studios towards the entrance of the semi-detached house on the left.

On the one hand, this reduction to bare essentials goes along with an opening towards the street: there is no hiding behind tall hedges or front-garden planting. On the other hand, the houses are closed towards the entrance side. The semi-detached houses open to the street only through the stairwell and studio windows. The fact that the studios so prominently dominate the entrance façade is, for one thing, due to the need to provide the artists with even light from the north for their work (the street is to the north of the houses). At the same time, however, this can surely be read as a programmatic statement: the studio was and still is the most important space in the Masters' Houses.

This is impressively confirmed during a tour of the interior. On the ground floor, the vestibule is followed by a small hallway which has six doors. On one side of the staircase are a vestibule, toilet and small chamber; on the other, a servery leading to the kitchen and into the basement, and a dining room; and, finally, the door to the living room, which is by far the largest room on the ground floor. The windows and doors of the dining and living rooms open to the garden and the sunny side, with an L-shaped terrace linking the two more formal rooms with the servery and kitchen.

The ground floor is thus dominated by small spatial volumes with many doors – something that was not particularly innovative even at the time. Yet in planning the houses, great importance was attached to a rational sequence of rooms which, together with the technologically innovative features, was intended to facilitate smooth, efficient housekeeping. The servery exemplifies how this aspiration was realised.

The kitchen, servery and dining room are arranged in a row in order to organise the work sequence of cooking, food arranging or serving and washing-up in the most obvious and labour-saving way possible. The servery and dining room are connected not just by a door: a built-in cabinet in the wall could be used from both sides. And the servery opens up yet another axis: from the terrace through the servery into the basement. Today, we would probably do without the separating walls, and the various processes of daily life would take place in a large, open-plan kitchen. Gropius, however, planned the sequence of separate, function-specific rooms of the Masters' Houses for a middle-class household with domestic staff: a housemaid providing household assistance, while the housing estate's caretaker serviced the heating system and was able to reach the basement unseen via the servery.

On the first floor are three bedrooms, a bathroom, a toilet and the studio. The bathroom connects two of the bedrooms. If we include the door from the hallway, this small room alone has three doors. Our impression of the ground floor is thus confirmed one floor higher: small spatial volumes with many doors. All the more impressive in its appearance is the studio as the centre of the artist's residence. By far the largest space, it lays claim to importance not least through a higher ceiling and the aforementioned studio window facing north, which is visible from the street.

Like the terrace on the ground floor, a wrap-around, L-shaped balcony connects two of the three bedrooms to the studio and, at least in summer, provides additional access points and connections. One of the pair of semi-detached houses has two additional bedrooms with access to the roof terrace on the second floor. The masters with children lived here. The other half of the house also had access to a roof terrace. Light, air and sun – this is what Neues Bauen (New Building) stood for, as it aimed to offer people better living conditions than in the nineteenth-century tenements. Light, air and sun also characterise the garden sides of the Masters' Houses, with their windows and doors, terraces and balconies, especially in contrast to the closed street side.

A TOUR OF THE HOUSING ESTATE

For all the democratisation efforts during the Weimar Republic, hierarchy was preserved in the architecture of the Masters' Houses. The director's residence is not a semi-detached house but a detached mansion, with a garage for the director's automobile instead of the low bicycle garage one finds in front of the other Masters' Houses. Unlike those of the semi-detached houses, the garden here is hidden from view, a wall having been erected in place of the wire-mesh fence. Yet, ironically, it was the upper-class director's mansion which was presented to the public upon completion as a prototype of new, democratic building and living in films, photographs and numerous publications.

In the history of modernist architecture, the Dessau Masters' Houses also occupy a central place because they so effectively presented the modern attitude towards living in various media. As a result, they became a symbol of modern residential architecture. Walter and Ise Gropius contributed very early on to the media propagation of the Dessau Masters' Houses, shying away neither from views into their private living spaces nor from retouching. In October 1926, for example, Ise Gropius gave the Dessau Housewives' Association a guided tour of the house to demonstrate the functional and efficient organisation of the home. Thousands of visitors toured the Gropius House in the years 1926–28 alone, when Walter and Ise Gropius lived there. The fourth chapter of the nine-part film *Wie wohnen wir gesund und wirtschaftlich?* (1926–28; How to live healthily and economically) presented to a wider public the modern amenities of the Dessau director's residence. Ise Gropius, her sister and a friend demonstrated in front of the camera the technical features and organisational achievements which were primarily intended to help housewives save time.

If one walks across the housing estate from the Seven Pillars to the Amaliensitz, the director's residence is followed by the semi-detached houses of László Moholy-Nagy and Lucia Moholy and of Lyonel and Julia Feininger, then by the semi-detached houses of Georg and El Muche and of Oskar and Tut Schlemmer and, finally, by the pair of semi-detached houses which were built for Wassily and Nina Kandinsky and for Paul and Lily Klee. Today, the houses are still named after this first crop of residents, even though some, such as Georg and El Muche, lived there only briefly; after they left, other Bauhäusler moved into their Dessau semi-detached house. Yet in terms of furnishings, not many traces are left of the first residents or subsequent tenants. This is due to the history of their use after the National Socialists forced the Bauhaus to close in Dessau in 1932.

Many pictures from the 1920s have survived, especially of the Gropius and Moholy-Nagy Houses, both of which were destroyed during World War II. It was these pictures that displayed a modern attitude towards living and gave the houses their significance for the history of architecture. As part of the historic renovation of the preserved Masters' Houses, many of the well-placed details and the colour design have also been restored, including the golden wall in the living room of Wassily Kandinsky and the black bedroom in the residence of Georg Muche. Even though the rooms are rather small and, from today's perspective, conventional in their arrangement, the colours continue to impress, as they add another dimension to what is perceived as monotonously white, functional modernism. Multicoloured was, as we know, Gropius's favourite colour.

THE MASTERS' HOUSES AFTER 1932

After Joost Schmidt and Helene Nonné-Schmidt, the last of the Bauhäusler, had left the Masters' House Settlement in 1933, the city of Dessau, which still owned the housing estate, let the houses to senior staff of the Junkers aircraft and engine works. Since there were no longer any artists living in the houses, and heating the houses had been difficult even in the previous years, the studios were repurposed for residential use. The large window surfaces were removed and replaced by smaller, conventional windows. This exterior alteration was at the same time exemplary of the rejection of modernism by the National Socialists. It was not the only alteration the buildings suffered: many others would follow.

On 7 March 1945, the director's residence and the semi-detached house of Moholy-Nagy were destroyed during the bombing of the city of Dessau. The rubble was removed and in 1956, a single-family home in the common style of the early GDR, with a traditional vocabulary of forms and a pitched roof, was built on top of the preserved souterrain of the director's residence. The Moholy-Nagy House was not subsequently replaced; at its site, a gap yawned in the ensemble of the Masters' House Settlement. The other semi-detached houses continued to be used for residential purposes and were, in some cases, repeatedly altered. Over the decades, the automobile garage in front of the Gropius House was the only building of the Masters' House Settlement that was largely preserved in its original state of 1926; on the other hand, the adjoining wall enclosing the garden was almost completely removed around 1965.

After German reunification, in the period from 1990 until 2002, the two preserved pairs of semi-detached houses and the one semi-detached house were renovated, and the green areas and tree population were eventually also restored according to preservationist principles. In 1996, the Masters' Houses were included in the list of UNESCO World Heritage sites. Since the completion in 2014 of the so-called New Masters' Houses – that is to say, the reinterpretation of the Gropius and Moholy-Nagy Houses by the architecture office of Bruno Fioretti Marquez – the entire Masters' House Settlement has belonged to the Bauhaus Dessau Foundation and been made open to the public.

The Masters' Houses stand among pine trees which
already dominated the plot of land at the time of
construction in 1925–26. A care concept was developed
to preserve the scene of white cubes among pines.

While the director had an automobile garage in front of his mansion, the semi-detached houses had only small bicycle garages. A discreet fence separated the more public area in front of the houses from the more private garden areas in the rear part of the plot.

Very few of the furnishings of the Masters' Houses survive, but
successful building research made it possible to largely restore the
colour scheme of the walls to its original condition. Highlights are the
colourful stairwells in the Muche House (left) and the "golden wall" in
the Kandinsky House (right).

The studio of the Schlemmer House (left) once again has artists working in it as part of the Bauhaus Residency Programme. The colour design here could not be restored, unlike the built-in cupboard in the Feininger House (top) or the bedroom of the Muche House (bottom).

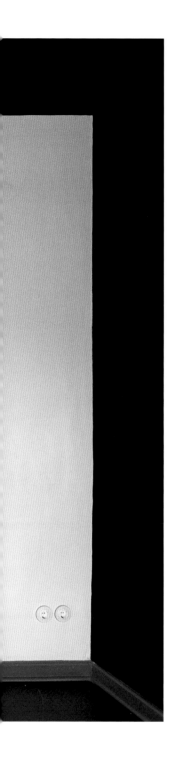

The so-called black bedroom in the Muche House (left) is based on a design by Marcel Breuer but did not meet with Georg Muche's approval. Compared with the other Masters' Houses, the colours in the Schlemmer House are generally somewhat more low-key – the bluish green of this door is unusual for the colour design of the Bauhaus buildings.

Vivid colours were selected for the design of the
Feininger House, including in the stairwell with access to
the roof terrace (left) and in one of the smaller bedrooms
on the first floor (right), where an original built-in
cupboard is preserved.

NEW MASTERS' HOUSES

BRUNO FIORETTI MARQUEZ 2011–14

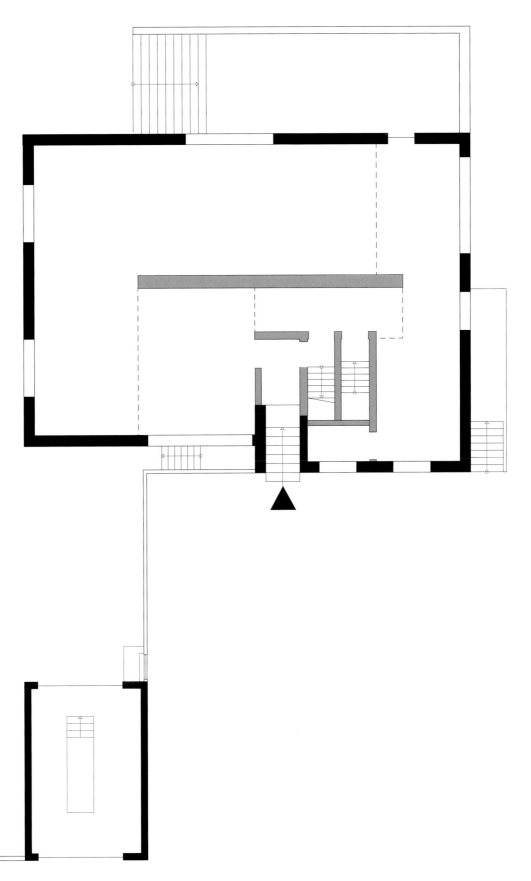

Gropius House, 2014:
ground floor

With its design for the New Masters' Houses, the architecture office of Bruno Fioretti Marquez has made a noteworthy contribution to the issue of reconstruction. Through the use of contemporary materials and the omission of historical details, the New Masters' Houses already signal on the very outside that they are neither original nor pretending to be. They do nonetheless restore the overall appearance of the ensemble of Masters' Houses lost during World War II. In 2015, the architects received the DAM Prize for Architecture in Germany for this repair of the complex and the exemplary, "imprecise" reconstruction of the Gropius and Moholy-Nagy Houses, which were destroyed in 1945, not least because their design reflects the distance to the past and yet leaves it visible.

THE DEBATE

Over the past two decades, debates have continued in many places in Germany about the reconstruction of buildings destroyed during World War II. Whether it is the city palace in Braunschweig or the one in Berlin or, more recently, Frankfurt's historic city centre, they usually involve the most detailed reconstruction possible of pre-modern building envelopes. Today's use, however, is invariably quite distinct from that of the original building. As a result of this discrepancy between outer shell and interior configuration, there is an inherent façade-like quality to such reconstructions.

The situation was similar for the Masters' Houses in Dessau, even though they are not pre-modern buildings but rather icons of modernism. The scale of the construction project was also much smaller than in the case of, say, palace reconstructions, as just a part of the ensemble was concerned.

In 2002, the renovation of the surviving five Masters' Houses was completed. That same year, the city acquired the Emmer House, which had been built in 1956 on top of the basement of the destroyed Gropius House. It had been privately owned for decades. With the acquisition, a debate began about what to do with the destroyed Moholy-Nagy and Gropius Houses. This debate lasted well over a decade. Should they be reconstructed or not? And if reconstruction was favoured, should the Emmer House consequently be knocked down in order to rebuild the Gropius House? Or was the Emmer House itself not a document of the way the GDR dealt with the legacy of the Bauhaus, making it a part of history and thus worth preserving?

In 2007, the city of Dessau eventually decided to organise a two-phase competition aimed at a repair of the entire complex of the Masters' Houses rather than a detailed reconstruction. The interiors of the New Masters' Houses were to be usable for events and exhibitions. As had been the case with other recent reconstruction projects, there was a conflict between exterior and interior. The shell was to be reconstituted but not reconstructed, but reverting to the original residential use was not thought feasible. Even the surviving historical Masters' Houses are today partly used for museum purposes.

THE DESIGN

The New Masters' Houses comprise the Moholy-Nagy and Gropius Houses, which are reconstructed only in their volume, as well as the wall around the garden of the Gropius House and the Trinkhalle (kiosk) by Ludwig Mies van der Rohe integrated into that wall, which were also reconstructed. The historical remains of the Gropius House – the automobile garage, the souterrain and a segment of the wall between the two – were incorporated into this overarching repair.

Standing in front of the Moholy-Nagy/Feininger double house, the rift between old and new, between historical and reconstructed shows as a vertical line. This straight line is obviously fictive: the fracture line following the impact of the bombs in World War II never ran straight like that. But this fictionality of the model division of the entire complex is part of the concept of Bruno Fioretti Marquez. In our memory, objects lose their details and become blurred. The architects put this observation into practice in their concept.

When comparing, the reconstructed Moholy-Nagy House standing on the left along the fictive, perfectly straight fracture line with the historical, renovated Feininger House on the right, what catches the eye are the consequences of an architecture of imprecision. Details of the original were largely dispensed with: no window sills or window partitions, no sheet-metal roof flashing or parapet covers. Walking around the Moholy-Nagy House, one does not see any gutters, terrace railings, lamps or mountings either. The new buildings appear monolithic and model-like. The windows are not only designed without details, but also semi-opaque yet translucent. The glass panes sit in narrow, black frames which are hardly recognisable as such and placed flush with the concrete façade. Instead of a white plaster surface, the entire visible structure is covered in the even grey of smooth exposed insulating concrete.

Yet creating these detail-less monoliths required a lot of detail work on the part of the architects and construction companies. What looks so simple is, in fact, highly complex and can be achieved only with a great deal of effort. The exposed insulating concrete, to give just one example, received a glaze in order to harmonise grey gradations in the concrete, lighten its dark colour, sharpen the edges, repair production-related damage and hide the anchor holes of the formwork.

When one enters the Moholy-Nagy or Gropius House, the distance to the lost original is strikingly apparent. Since the houses are no longer used as residences, the original fragmented floor plans could be dispensed with in this overarching repair of the ensemble. Bruno Fioretti Marquez instead created a sculpture of space: a single flowing space across two or three levels, which has liberated itself from Gropius's original to provide a contemporary continuous hall for events and exhibitions.

Yet similar to the exterior, the architects want the interior of the New Masters' Houses to be understood as a reference to the historical Masters' Houses, bring inside and outside together and thereby avoid the façade-like character of many reconstructions. In many of the Dessau buildings by Walter Gropius, built-in closets constitute a central theme of sorts. The sculpture of space brought into the frame, a timber post construction, of the New Masters' Houses accommodates the stairs, the lift and the technical installations – in the same way that a closet accommodates clothes and all sorts of possessions one wishes to hide from view. The plaster surfaces of the sculpture of space – an artwork with the French title *Le pigment de la lumière* created by the artist Olaf Nicolai – also reference the colourful surface decoration of the historical buildings and bring the dialogue between architecture and art up to date.

Like the Feininger House, the Moholy-Nagy House is used on a long-term basis by the Kurt Weill Society. The Gropius House is used by the Bauhaus Dessau Foundation as a visitor centre for the historical Masters' Houses and as an exhibition space for contemporary art. As part of the garden wall, the Trinkhalle, the only building in Dessau designed by the third and last Bauhaus director, Ludwig Mies van der Rohe, was also recreated. During the summer months, the new Trinkhalle is a popular café.

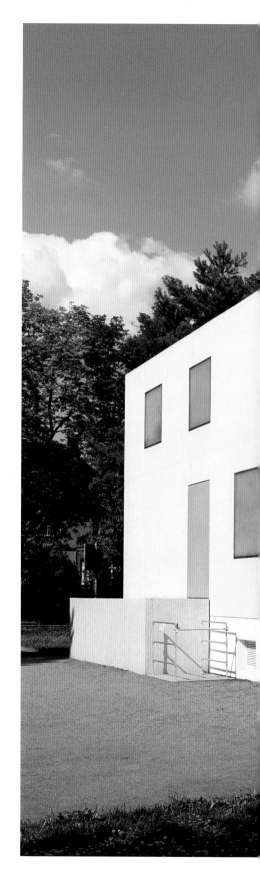

At the rear of the Gropius House, one can clearly see how
the abstracted new building contrasts with the surviving
basement. Structurally, the cantilevered section on the
first floor of the building was not feasible back in 1926.
Gropius embraced the pillars and covered them with
mirrors to make them visually disappear.

While the exterior of the new Gropius House draws on the original, this approach was abandoned in the interior in favour of an impressive space and exhibition area (right). The automobile garage of the director's mansion is preserved in its original state (bottom left), while Mies van der Rohe's Trinkhalle (kiosk) underwent a contemporary interpretation.

Here, one can clearly see the intersection between the historical Masters' Houses and the so-called New Masters' Houses: while the Feininger House (right) was preserved and renovated, the Moholy-Nagy House (left) was destroyed by a bomb in 1945.

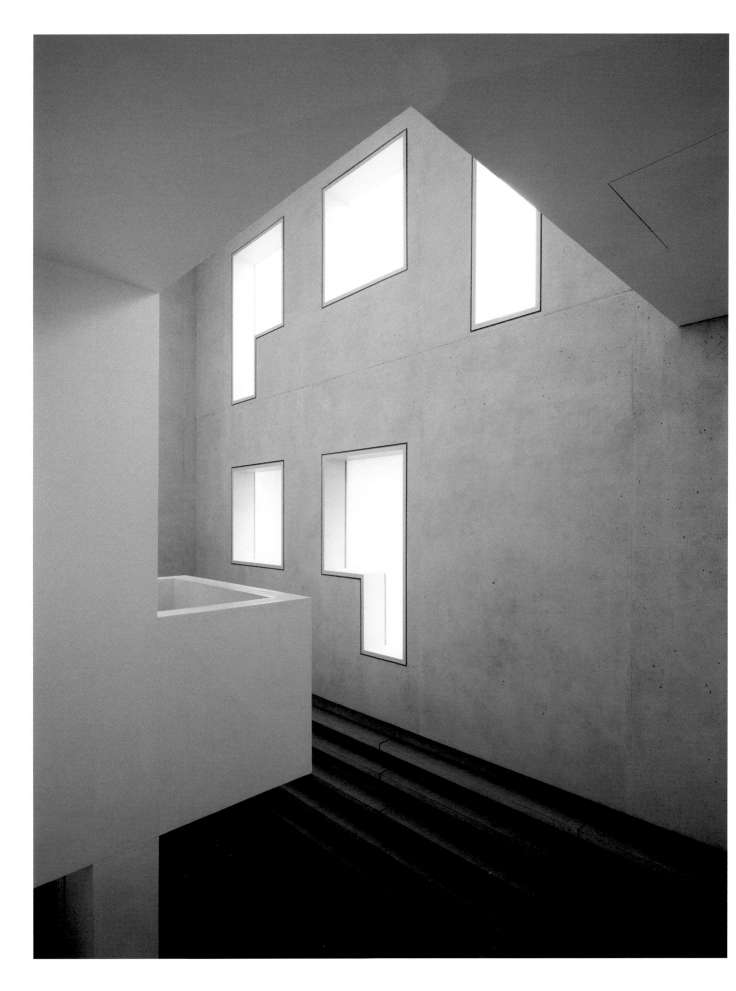

Inside and out, the surfaces of the New Masters' Houses
are grey insulating exposed concrete, which contrasts
with the colour design of the historical Masters' Houses.
The historical floor plan was abandoned for both the
Gropius House and the Moholy-Nagy House.

THE NAURATH AND HAHN HOUSES

RICHARD PAULICK
1928

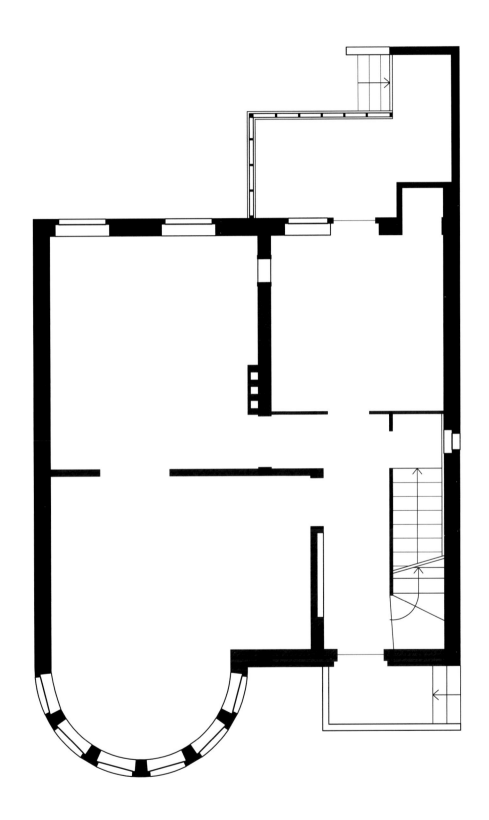

Hahn House:
ground floor

Located in a residential area to the south-west of the Bauhaus Building and within walking distance of it are the Naurath and Hahn Houses. Together with the nearby houses that Friedrich Engemann built on Fischereiweg and Stephanweg, they add middle-class residences for private clients to the Dessau Bauhaus buildings. After all, the city of Dessau had commissioned construction of the Masters' Houses in the vicinity as artist residences, and the Dessau-Törten Housing Estate as inexpensive mass housing.

Ernst Naurath and Albert Hahn were the clients of the two detached single-family homes on Kiefernweg. It is not entirely clear, however, who was responsible for their design. Richard Paulick, who worked in the architecture office of Walter Gropius from 1928 until 1930, is regarded as the architect, for it was he who signed the construction plans. Yet we also know of an unrealised alternative design for the Hahn House which bears the stamp "bauhaus-dessau bauabteilung" and the signature of Hans Wittwer, who taught in the Building Department from 1927 until 1929.

Both houses have two storeys and an almost square floor plan with a flat roof. The two structures differ only in the orientation of the single-storey, half-round extension and in some details. The extension of the Naurath House is on the garden side, while that of the Hahn House is on the street side. The street-facing façade of the Naurath House is staggered inward slightly towards the entrance, whereas the Hahn House has a conservatory addition on the garden side.

Unlike the Naurath House, the Hahn House suffered only relatively minor modifications after it was built. Many original details are still preserved, including the windows, which are arranged in ribbons and emphasise horizontality, as was typical of New Building; the flush-closing wooden doors with the Gropius-designed door handles; and the radiators in the living room. The balcony balustrade above the round street-side extension, however, was changed at a later time, amounting to what may be the most serious alteration of the original structure: instead of horizontally mounted steel tubes (as seen to this day on the Masters' Houses), a parapet was built.

The Hahn House had two rooms and a kitchen with pantry and conservatory addition on the ground floor, and three rooms plus bathroom on the upper floor. The bathroom can be identified from the outside by the narrow skylight above the entrance. The basement provided space for a utility room, cellar storeroom, smoking chamber and henhouse.

The Naurath and Hahn Houses are still occupied today and therefore not open to the public.

The exterior of the Hahn House has changed little since it was built. The most significant change here is the parapet built around the roof terrace in place of the original delicate metal railing.

Much is preserved inside the Hahn House too, including the windows and radiators seen here in the round window bay facing the street (left) and the doors with the characteristic Gropius-designed door handles. The Naurath House (right) saw more significant changes, such as the installation of new plastic-frame windows.

THE ENGEMANN HOUSE AND THE GROUP OF HOUSES ON FISCHEREIWEG/ STEPHANWEG

FRIEDRICH ENGEMANN 1930–33

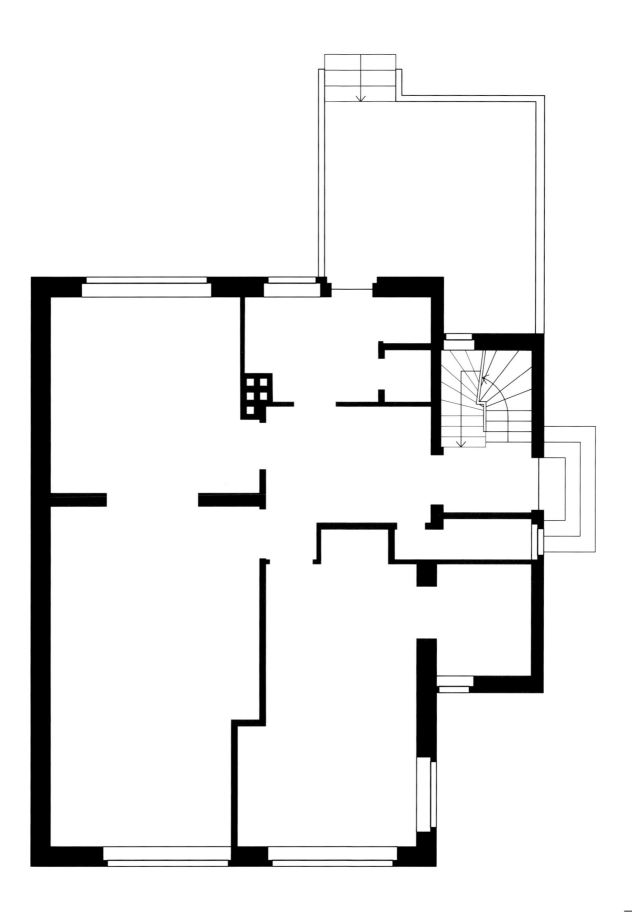

Engemann House:
ground floor

In the area between the Bauhaus Building and the Masters' Houses, Friedrich Engemann built a group of residences which, like the nearby Naurath and Hahn Houses by Richard Paulick, were designed for middle-class living. Unlike the Paulick residences, however, the group of houses on Fischereiweg/Stephanweg is moderately or conservatively modernist. Engemann's residences thus remind us today that modernism and the Bauhaus could take many forms and included multiple styles and nuances which can not only be linked to the Bauhaus's three directors, but are also clearly evident in the Bauhaus architecture of Dessau.

After studying at the Bauhaus, Friedrich Engemann, a trained mason, was hired in 1929 to teach architectural drawing, interior design and descriptive geometry at the Bauhaus. As the deputy of Ludwig Mies van der Rohe, the third Bauhaus director, he also temporarily acted as head of the Building and Extension Department. During this time, he also built his own residence at Fischereiweg 24 and the adjacent homes at Fischereiweg 20, 22 and 26, as well as at Stephanweg 1. The Bauhaus workshops were involved in the interior design of these houses

Engemann's residence is detached and placed with the short side facing the street. This is striking, as the other houses of the group are conceived as semi-detached houses with their short sides facing the adjacent neighbouring buildings. Common to all houses is a traditional hip roof with eaves board, roof overhang and dormers (or a gabled roof at Stephanweg 1). Contrary to what one might expect when comparing the predominantly flat-roofed other Bauhaus structures with these residences, these roofs were not added at a later time.

Most of the details pointing to Bauhaus architecture and New Building have been lost over the decades as a result of various renovations and modifications. The street-facing windows, for instance, had a landscape format and, moreover, were connected to a stripe of dark plaster within the otherwise brightly plastered façade to form horizontal bands running all the way around the corners of the structures. Emphasising horizontality in this manner, the houses by Friedrich Engemann expressly referred to a main element of modern building.

Engemann organised the interiors of the houses in a functional and clear way; his own house featured two apartments. The functional fixtures and furniture, which he also designed, were characteristic of Bauhaus furnishings. The desk for his own house, for example, stood on tubular steel runners and, in this, is reminiscent of classic designs by Marcel Breuer and other Bauhäusler.

The Engemann family lived in the house at Fischereiweg 24 until 1950. Today, it accommodates a dental practice and an apartment. The other Engemann-built houses on Fischereiweg and Stephanweg are used to this day as residences and therefore not publicly accessible.

Today, the private residence of Friedrich Engemann is no longer readily recognisable as a Bauhaus building. This is due to the new windows and roof tiles as well as the selected colour scheme. The roof shape, however, was not altered.

The other buildings in this group of houses also still feature the original, conservatively modernist roof types. Of this pair of semi-detached houses on Stephanweg (top right), the one on the right comes closest to conveying an impression of the original state.

KORNHAUS
RESTAURANT

CARL FIEGER
1929/30

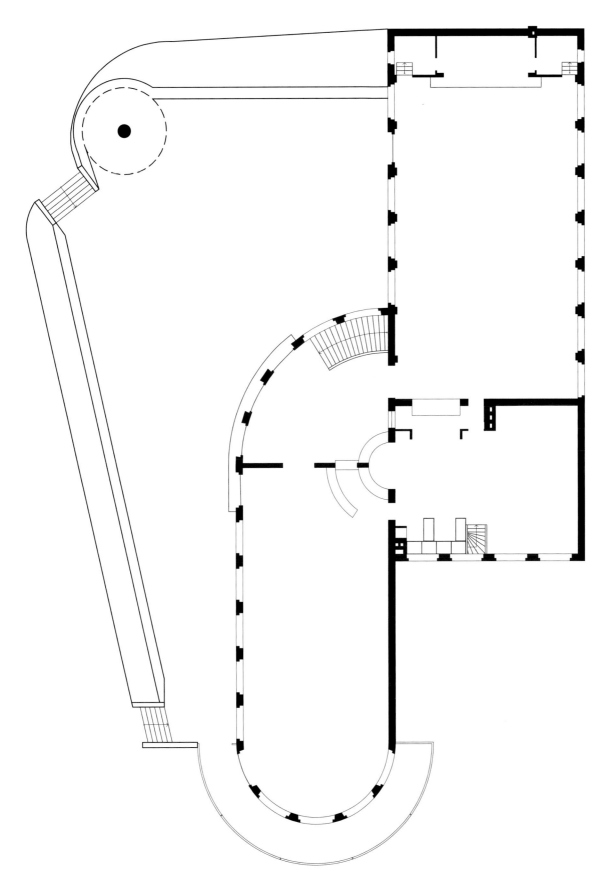

Embankment level

The Kornhaus Restaurant is located in the very north of Dessau at a loop of the River Elbe in the district of Ziebigk. With this building, Carl Fieger offered proof that the modern architecture of the Bauhaus could not only be realised in the open, flat field – as in the case with the Bauhaus Building and the Dessau-Törten Housing Estate – but also sensitively fit into a landscape of outstanding natural beauty and great recreational value.

BACKGROUND

Until the 1870s, a granary stood on the site of the restaurant, which had been replaced by Fieger's Kornhaus in 1930 – "Kornhaus" is the German word for granary. Right next to the granary was a steamboat pier which brought day trippers and probably contributed to the decision in favour of this building site. At the adjacent Leopoldshafen harbour, a boathouse of the Junkers steel construction company was also built in 1930, which added yet another aspect to the recreational activities at this bend in the River Elbe.

In 1929, the city of Dessau, together with the Schultheiss-Patzenhofer Brewery, had launched a competition for the planned restaurant. Against competitors such as the then Bauhaus director Hannes Meyer, who participated together with the Bauhaus Building Department, Carl Fieger was able to prevail with his design under his own name.

From 1921 until 1934, Fieger was one of the most important associates in the private architecture office of Walter Gropius. As such, he was substantially involved in many of the firm's seminal building designs, such as the Bauhaus Building. From 1927 to 1930, he also taught architectural drawing and descriptive geometry as part of architectural theory at the Bauhaus Dessau. In 1926, he began to do independent work in addition to his activities for Gropius's office, realising under his own name the Kornhaus Restaurant and his own residence in Dessau-Törten in the years before the Bauhaus in Dessau closed.

DESIGN

With its two storeys, the Kornhaus nestles against the Elbe embankment. From the street, the building presents itself as a two-storey structure, whereas from the embankment only the upper level with its flat roof is visible. As you enter the building on the street level, the ladies' and men's rooms are to the left and right of the porch. The porch leads to the cloakroom area, from which one reaches the bar on the right and various ancillary rooms on the left. In the left half of the building, the latter are grouped around the walled courtyard.

A spacious, elegantly curved staircase leads up from the cloakroom area to the embankment level. The curve of the staircase corresponds to the quadrant of the upstairs vestibule and runs below the windows along the outer wall to the terrace. The vestibule is the central hub for the entire level. From there, one reaches the street-side hall with a stage, the riverside guest area with its glazed, semicircular terrace and, finally, a large open terrace on the embankment with the distinctive concrete Tanzpilz ("dance mushroom"). The two oblong structures for the hall and guest area were offset from one another, so that the terrace was also accessible from the hall.

The kitchen is located in the corner between the hall and the guest area and looks out onto the courtyard. It has its own staircase connecting it to the utility rooms on the street level. It was positioned at the junction of the two oblong structures in such a way that food and drinks can be provided directly – via a semicircular counter and a bar adjacent to it – to both the guest area and the vestibule with the open terrace

The curved forms of the floor plan may be due to the functionally organised restaurant operations: the spaces flow almost imperceptibly from one into the other, enabling a smooth operation. On the other hand, Fieger took up the forms of nature at the river for various curves (half- and quarter-circles), specifically the river loop at which the building is located. It seems almost as if he had sought to reconcile nature and the building with the help of geometry, or to translate nature into strict geometry. The glazed semicircle of the guest area extends over the embankment towards the Elbe like a cruise ship. And like a statement explaining this method, the full circle in the form of the concrete-cast Tanzpilz stands at the other end of the terrace overlooking the landscape.

Various design details further underscore the dynamic effect of flowing, such as in the rounded edges in the entrance area on the street side or in the bar. Although a vertical format was chosen for the wood-frame windows in the white-rendered façade, they, too, convey a dynamism by being divided horizontally and combined into a ribbon through narrow, continuous sills. In addition to these details, the architect also designed crucial elements of the interior decoration, which in many ways refers to other Bauhaus buildings. These include the colour scheme, which accentuates the visible construction – a reinforced concrete skeleton with masonry infills. A similar colour scheme can still be seen in the Bauhaus Building today. The globe lights by Marianne Brandt are yet another reference to the Bauhaus, as is the clear red lettering on the building.

Thanks to renovation work carried out in 1996 and 2012, the Kornhaus is largely in its original state, offering us insights into much of the historical architecture and the original design ideas. To this day, the building is used as a restaurant.

Carl Fieger sensitively placed the restaurant into the Elbe River landscape. From the river, one sees only the upper of the two floors. The semicircular glazed terrace gives the building the look of a pavilion from one side (left). Located on the other side of the restaurant is the Tanzpilz (right).

Much of the inside is preserved or has been restored. The semicircular glazed terrace in the west offers a view of the Elbe landscape (left). The hall and its stage (top right) have regained their original radiant colouring. Lighting is provided by lamps designed by Marianne Brandt. The seating is not original.

Both floors can be seen from the street side (large image). The basement level houses, among other things, a bar (top left). The blue colour of the window frames and doors is consistent with Fieger's design.

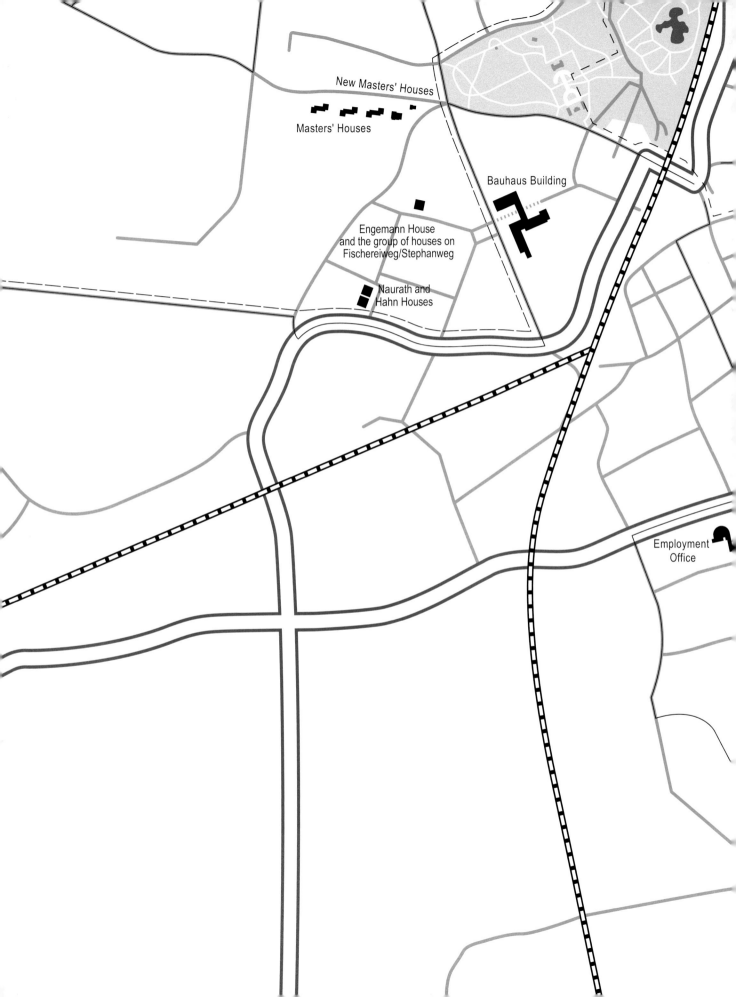

New Masters' Houses

Masters' Houses

Bauhaus Building

Engemann House
and the group of houses on
Fischereiweg/Stephanweg

Naurath and
Hahn Houses

Employment
Office

EMPLOYMENT OFFICE

WALTER GROPIUS 1928/29

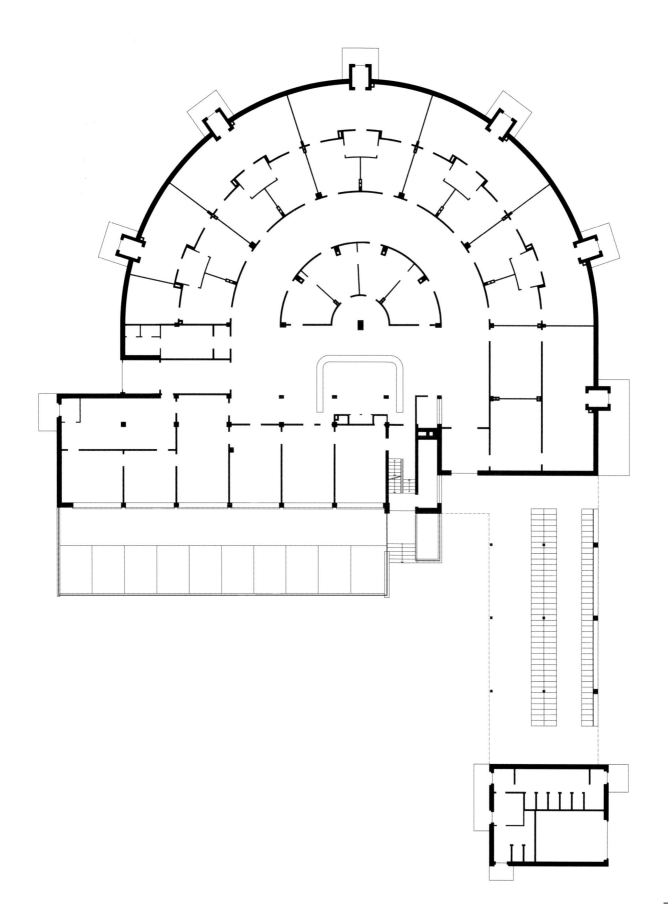

Ground floor

The employment office as a distinct building type posed a new construction challenge in the 1920s. The Reichsanstalt für Arbeitsvermittlung und Arbeitslosenversicherung (Reich Institute for Labour Placement and Unemployment Insurance) was founded in 1927 against the backdrop of the industrial society and mass unemployment during the Weimar Republic. The existing employment office buildings, which had been under local administration, proved increasingly inadequate as a result of the expanded tasks and responsibilities of the now state-run employment offices and the high number of unemployed using their services. The Dessau Employment Office by Walter Gropius is one of the early examples of the new building type. With its semicircular low-rise building and the two-storey administrative wing, Gropius managed to combine maximum rationalisation of the interior organisation with the greatest possible architectural elegance.

BACKGROUND

With the creation of the Reich Institute for Labour Placement and Unemployment Insurance and the large-scale unemployment in the wake of the worldwide economic crisis from 1929 on, the newly erected employment offices were seen as an architectural manifestation of the sociopolitical aspirations of the Weimar Republic. They were buildings of great importance to the cities, and in numerous places the architectural solutions were, as a result, prestigious, or at least there were calls for representative buildings. In historical retrospect, it is perhaps not surprising, therefore, that Gropius's Employment Office remained the only Bauhaus structure in the centre of Dessau – even if it left much to be desired in terms of representativeness and its qualities focused instead on other aspects of architectural expression.

The central office of the Reich Institute for Labour Placement and Unemployment Insurance was located in Berlin. In the organisational structure, it was followed by thirteen state employment offices and, finally, the 361 employment offices of the German Reich. As early as 1923 – that is, even before the founding of the Reich Institute – there were first efforts in Dessau to have a new building constructed for one of those employment offices. For this reason, the city launched a restricted competition. A study for employment office buildings by Martin Wagner, head of the Berlin planning and building control office, which had been commissioned by the Reichsarbeitsverwaltung (Reich Labour Administration), served as the design brief for the architects Hugo Häring, Max Taut and Walter Gropius, who were invited to participate in 1927.

The site chosen for the new building of the Dessau Employment Office was Askanischer Platz, an originally peripheral square which had become central as a result of rapid urban growth. Unlike today, it was a triangular site which had been designed mainly as a green space, with a gymnasium and playground for the neighbouring primary school. Directly to the south of it was the Neuer Begräbnisplatz, a municipal cemetery of high architectural quality, which the architect Friedrich Wilhelm von Erdmannsdorff had built just outside the city gates in 1787–79. In his plans, Gropius seized on the enclosing wall of the cemetery with regard to the alignment as well as the material (brick) of the Dessau Employment Office.

DESIGN

In his design for the Employment Office, Gropius arrived at a fascinating balance of asymmetrically arranged building parts, each of which give shape to a particular function. This had also been the case two years previously with his design for the Bauhaus Building. But while the various parts of the Bauhaus Building form an extensive arrangement covering much of the building site, the different parts of the Employment Office are arranged more closely together owing to the narrow central urban site.

The parts of the building include the following: the semicircular low-rise building with various separate employment service spaces for women and men and for particular occupational categories; the two-storey building for the administration; the single-storey, elongated low-rise building for bicycles and toilet facilities; and the stairwell, which is highlighted as a distinct building volume.

The building sections were arranged in such a way that the administrative wing and the elongated low-rise building were placed at right angles to one another and framed the playground (no longer existent) located to the south. In this context, the stairwell with its tower-like shape serves as a compositional anchor of sorts. The entrance to the administration leads through the stairwell, but involves passing a short bridge across the ditch and embankment, which allows for natural illumination of the lower level of the administrative wing. This bridge stages the entrance and lends it, for all its modesty, a representative appearance.

The semicircular low-rise building with its characteristic saw-tooth roof is attached to the administrative wing on the north side and extends into the tip of the triangular site, but does not completely cover it on account of the geometry of semicircle and triangle. Viewed from the north, the semicircular labour exchange wing is a kind of Kopfbau, or head-end structure, whose wall of yellow bricks forms a closed front for the viewer. Only the canopied entrance doors for the individual occupational groups opened up the wall. Lighting was provided exclusively by a narrow skylight strip and the glazed saw-tooth roof.

The spaces for the administration, occupational guidance and labour exchange with cash till area were clearly separated in order to avoid intersecting paths and unclear situations and thus contribute to a more efficiently designed work environment. When the Employment Office was completed and put into operation in 1929, job seekers entered the semicircular low-rise building through one of the doors based on their occupation and gender. Via an outer ring of waiting rooms, they reached the rooms of the particular placement officers in a second ring and finally, through a semicircular hallway again connecting all sections yet still separating men and women by means of a barrier, to the department of unemployment welfare and the cash till behind it in the centre of the building. Social protection by the state was thus the key programmatic concept of the building, which at the same time programmatically referenced modern industrial construction in some of its aspects: the steel skeleton-frame construction, the saw-tooth roof, the bricks of the exterior walls and the brightly glazed tiles of the interior walls in the public spaces.

AFTER 1929

The architectural quality of the Dessau Employment Office by Gropius lies in its exemplary synthesis of function, construction and design. In spite of this high standard, it was not used as a model in the subsequent construction of employment office buildings. It lost both its original use and a large part of its urban context.

As early as 1934, the semicircular low-rise building was no longer needed for labour placement and was repurposed for office space. In 1936, wood-frame windows were therefore set into the wall of the flat building, significantly changing its appearance. By 1932, the public toilet facilities had already been converted into a registration office, and in 1935 the bicycle shelter was enclosed to create additional spaces. Plans by the National Socialists to demolish the building, which they regarded as an abhorrent example of "cultural bolshevism", were thwarted by the war, and the Employment Office came to be one of the few architectural monuments in the city centre to survive the bombing of Dessau on 7 March 1945. After the war, the building was used by different administrative bodies and institutions.

Starting in 1967, the redevelopment of the city centre of Dessau in line with socialist modernism and its characteristic concrete-slab construction dramatically changed the surroundings of the Employment Office. The triangular Askanischer Platz was transformed into a rectangular open space between sets of five-storey row houses. Renamed August Bebel-Platz, it is now used partly as a public green space, partly as a parking lot. A twelve-storey apartment building erected behind the Employment Office almost dwarfs the historical structure.

Inside, however, much of the original structure has survived. Entering the building today, one is still surprised and impressed by the spaciousness, clarity and the abundance of light. Since its renovation in 2003, the building houses the Office for Public Order and Traffic of the city of Dessau-Roßlau.

The tripartite wooden windows in the semicircular head-end structure of the Employment Office were not installed until later. Furthermore, the windows were equipped with additional temporary frames in the course of renovation work. The tubular steel enclosure of the green area is also found in other Gropius-designed buildings in Dessau.

The administrative wing on the south side of the building offers not two but three floors of office space, as a spacious light shaft also provides sufficient light in the basement rooms.

The old lettering of the words "Amt für Arbeit" can still be seen on the stairwell. The semicircular saw-tooth roof, which is preserved largely in its original form, is particularly important for the building as a whole and its spatial effect.

Inside, all spaces are linked by the drop ceiling with its
thin steel trim and the skylights. The globe lights by
Marianne Brandt, which are also found in the Bauhaus
Building, would nowadays no longer be bright enough
for office work and were therefore replaced.

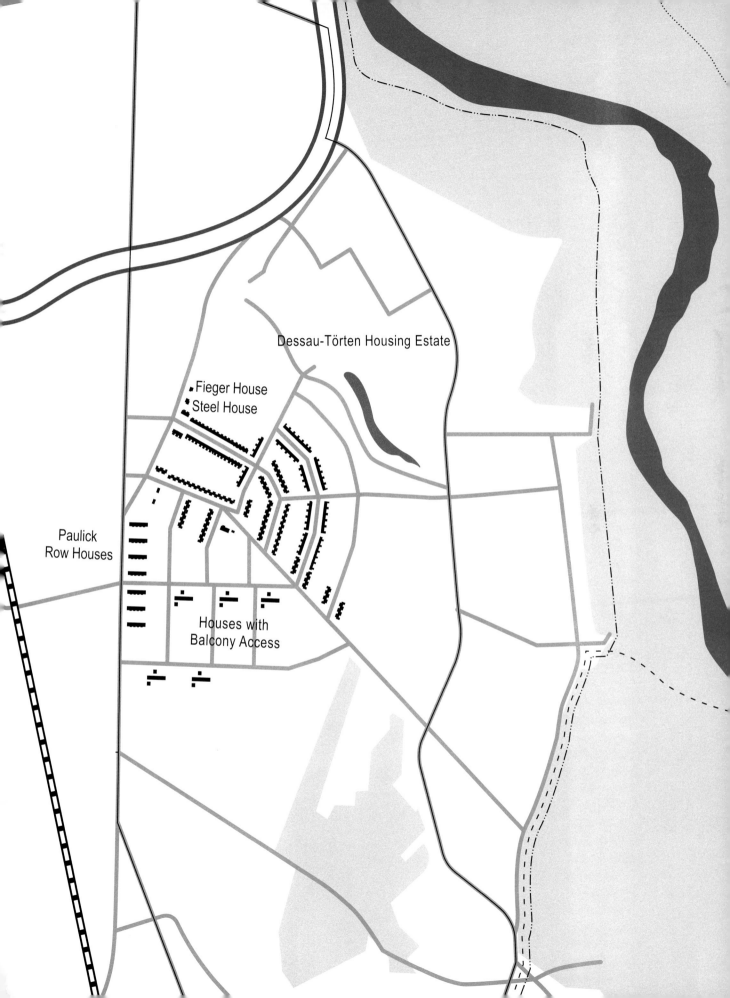

Dessau-Törten Housing Estate

Fieger House
Steel House

Paulick
Row Houses

Houses with
Balcony Access

DESSAU-TÖRTEN HOUSING ESTATE

WALTER GROPIUS
1926–28

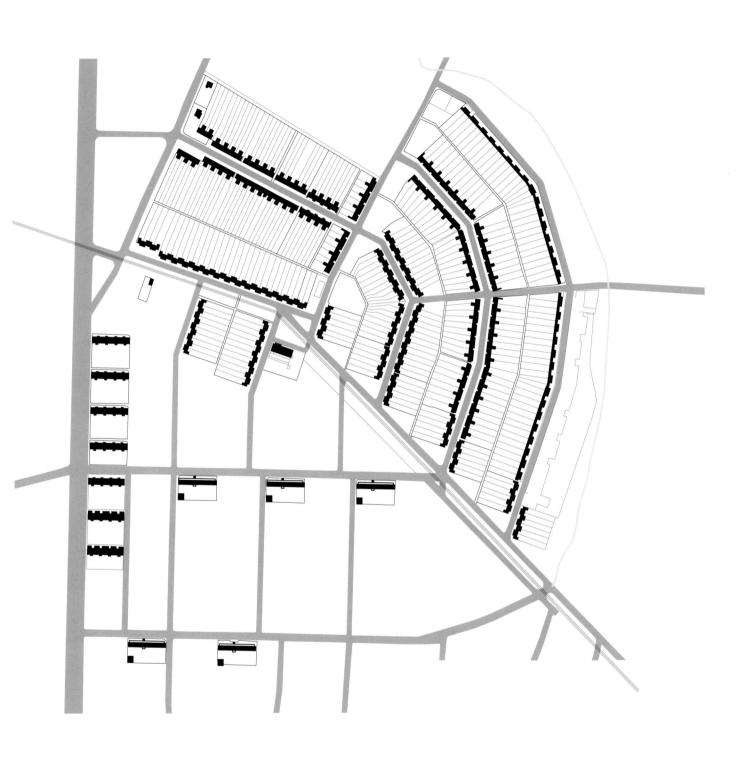

Plan of the Bauhaus buildings in
the Dessau-Törten Housing Estate

The Dessau-Törten Housing Estate was built in 1926–28 between the city of Dessau and the village of Törten according to plans by Walter Gropius and with the involvement of the Bauhaus workshops. The 314 realised terraced houses with their large kitchen gardens were Gropius's response to the issues that mass housing construction in the years after World War I raised for architects. More than in any other modernist housing estate, the rationalisation of the building process and construction became apparent in the architecture and design of the Dessau-Törten Housing Estate. An attempt was made here to wring a distinct aesthetic language from mass housing and create high-quality housing for workers in spite of the need to minimise costs. Ever since its completion in 1928, the housing estate has been part of the, at times, fiercely debated canon of modern housing development projects.

BACKGROUND

In 1925, the city of Dessau and its mayor, Fritz Hesse, had at least two good reasons to bid for a move of the Bauhaus to Dessau. For one thing, the school of design was already world-famous and would thus certainly raise the city's profile. For another, as an emerging industrial city in the 1920s, Dessau was in dire need of new housing for workers at the local industrial companies. With its innovative approaches to architecture and construction methods, the Bauhaus was expected to significantly contribute towards dealing with the housing shortage.

In June 1926, the city of Dessau therefore initially commissioned the construction of sixty homes under so-called Heimstätten (Home) law and on the basis of a concept previously developed by the private architecture office of Walter Gropius. The Reichsheimstätten Act of 1920 regulated the acquisition of fixed-use, fixed-price and specially protected ownership of a single-family home. The purpose of this law was to enable low-income families to acquire adequate housing and a plot of land for self-subsistence, while at the same time making it impossible for potential creditors to seize the land and the building on it.

In its programmatic conception, the Dessau-Törten Housing Estate therefore hardly compares to the kind of Bauhaus housing estate Gropius and other Bauhäusler had been envisioning since 1919. While plans from 1923 for a Bauhaus housing estate in Weimar do bear a certain formal resemblance to the first construction stage of the Dessau housing estate in terms of the urban planning concept – in both cases, for instance, the building lines of the terraced houses open up towards an implied, asymmetric square – what was needed in Dessau-Törten was not housing for Bauhaus teachers and students but affordable homes for Dessau residents.

This commission put Gropius and the Bauhaus in direct competition with other housing development projects in Dessau, some of them already built, while others were also under construction from 1926 on – such as the Dessau-Ziebigk garden housing estate by Leopold Fischer and Leberecht Migge, which, in its language of forms, is also associated with the New Building style. Perhaps even more than in the case of the Bauhaus Building and the Masters' Houses, the Bauhaus under Gropius needed to subject its ideas and concepts in Dessau-Törten to a reality check and, in doing so, hold its own among competing views of modernism.

TERRACED HOUSES AND SPECIAL STRUCTURES: 1926–28

Construction of the terraced houses based on plans by Gropius took place in three phases between 1926 and 1928. The first construction phase was begun in September 1926 and completed in the spring of 1927. Fifty-eight of the originally planned sixty terraced houses were realised, with two of the houses of the first construction phase already open for viewing by the time of the inauguration of the Bauhaus Building on 4 December 1926. On 11 May 1927, a second construction phase involving one hundred houses was commissioned by order of the Dessau city council, and on 17 February 1928, the council also finally approved the third and last construction phase involving an additional 156 houses. This final phase was completed the same year, while Gropius had already resigned as Bauhaus director.

The terrain of the housing estate is level and has favourable building ground, with sand and gravel providing the essential components for producing concrete on-site. Hence the decision to opt for concrete construction immediately suggested itself, if only because of the savings on transportation costs for part of the construction materials. The focus in the construction schedule and the overall planning and construction process was on rationalisation and cost-saving efforts. The floor plans and the construction method were planned in the most economical way, precise time schedules were drawn up for the various trades on the building lot, and the structural components were produced on-site in assembly line-like manner. Henry Ford's production methods for automobiles served as a model for this approach to rationalised construction.

The extended kitchen gardens behind the terraced houses and the location in what at the time was still a largely undeveloped landscape by the River Mulde made Gropius himself speak of a "semi-rural housing estate" (a type of housing estate which had by no means been invented by Gropius). Even in its layout, organised around a centre, the housing estate takes its cue from the garden city as it had been developed in England from the late nineteenth century on, and which was also propagated and realised in Germany to improve housing and living conditions.

The centre of the housing estate is marked by a pylon with the adjacent five-storey Konsum Building. The high-voltage line may be read as a symbol of progress and the embodiment of rationality, while the Konsum Building represents the social centre of the estate. As if viewing the high-tension pylon as the insertion point of a compass, the planners arranged the streets of the housing estate radially around it. Combined with the inserted access streets, the result is a spider web of sorts.

Three different basic types of housing estate houses (with a few variations) were realised in the three construction stages. Gropius used the acronym "SieTö" (for Siedlung Törten, or Törten Housing Estate) and the numbers I to IV to describe them, with SieTö III remaining unrealised. They differ in floor plan and elevation, construction and furnishings. The 1927 SieTö I and II-type houses are two-storey terraced houses which differ in a few details: the SieTö I-type houses are fully cellared, while a deep basement was dispensed with in the SieTö II-type houses because of the high groundwater level. The basement is accordingly smaller and shallower, with its floor just six steps below the ground floor. To make up for this, the SieTö II type has an additional bath on the upper floor and its plot size was widened by almost two metres (from 5.9 to 7.8 metres) to allow more cultivation compared with the SieTö I type.

The flat-roofed terraced houses consist of hollow cinder blocks produced on-site for the load-bearing walls and concrete joists also produced at the construction site for the ceiling. The non-load-bearing walls were filled in with various materials and the windows in steel frames were inserted directly underneath the ceilings in horizontal ribbons. The structural principle of the load-bearing cross-walls showed in the design of the façades, albeit in a visually abstracted form.

The additional funding for the housing estate structures in Dessau-Törten promised in 1928 by the Reichsforschungsgesellschaft für Wirtschaftlichkeit im Bau- und Wohnungswesen (Reich Research Association for Economic Efficiency in Building and Housing) was tied to the condition that an additional group of brick houses be constructed, in order to allow for a systematic analysis of factors such as cost, durability and warmth retention in comparison with the other concrete terraced houses. The houses built in traditional construction have the same floor plan as the II-type houses, but for all the similarity, their exteriors differ from those made of concrete, as they appear as homogeneous structures with punch windows.

All types have a very similar layout. On the ground floor, the entrance hallway with the staircase leads to the living room, the eat-in kitchen with sink unit and, in the attached stable, the Metroclo, a composting toilet developed by the garden architect Leberecht Migge. On the upper floor, there were three bedrooms (and another bathroom in the II-type house) and access to the roof terrace above the attached stable.

The IV-type house was created in 1928 as a split-level solution to accommodate rising construction costs and keep the price for a home around 10,000 Reichsmarks. The living area was reduced in this way from the 75 or 70 square metres of the previous types to 57 square metres, the split-level solution helping to organise this small living space. After passing through the entrance area, one immediately enters the living room, which, like the adjacent kitchen, is oriented towards the garden. As a connecting room, the living room also serves circulation purposes, providing access to the kitchen and, a few steps up, to the two bedrooms facing the street. Descending a half-staircase from the kitchen, one enters the low-ceilinged basement (with a ceiling height of 1.8 metres) underneath the bedrooms. In the IV-type house, the composting toilet is also located in the attached stable, which is likewise accessible from the kitchen.

In addition to the terraced houses, Gropius's architecture office planned a number of special structures for the housing estate. From 1929 on, the aforementioned Konsum Building, with the store of the consumers' cooperative on the ground floor, provided the residents of the housing estate with a first larger supply facility for everyday needs. The five-storey part of the building, moreover, housed three rental flats.

Since the sewage system of the entire housing estate was three metres below the level of the municipal sewage interceptor, sewage had to be pumped to the higher level. For this reason, the so-called pump station was built at the entrance to the estate along the high-voltage line in 1928. As early as the 1930s, however, the structure was used as a transformer station for the estate and extended in length by 2.6 metres for this purpose. A dairy shop planned across from the Konsum Building – as a semicircular structure projecting from the building line of the terraced houses – was never realised.

Experimental construction site and mass production of affordable housing are two conflicting functions, because possible construction flaws would automatically be repeated serially. While it had been possible to keep construction costs at a moderate level compared with other housing estates, it was not long before construction defects came to light. Following completion of the houses, numerous structural changes were made to correct the flaws. These included converting the windows (from horizontal ribbon windows with steel frames to small punch windows with wood frames) and cladding or painting the façades or raising protective walls in front of them. Gropius had effectively staged the organisation of the construction site and the desired rationalisation of the entire construction process with an eye to publicity – including through street names such as "Doppelreihe" ("double row") and "Kleinring" (small ring) – but what ultimately interested him most of all was the artistic interpretation of rationalisation.

AFTER 1928

When Gropius left the Bauhaus in 1928, Hannes Meyer took over as the second director of the school of design. Gropius's private architecture office continued to be involved in the Dessau-Törten Housing Estate into the year 1929 (to oversee the completion of the Konsum Building, among other things), but at the same time, the Building Department under the direction of Meyer began new planning efforts for an expansion of the housing estate. Subsequently, the Houses with Balcony Access and the row houses for the Deutsche Wohnungsfürsorge AG (DEWOG; German housing assistance for civil servants, employees and workers) were built according to plans by Richard Paulick. In 1930–31, Leopold Fischer – a student of the Viennese architect Adolf Loos, former associate in Gropius's architecture office and, from the mid-1920s on, one of his competitors in the Dessau housing development – added houses based on his own designs to a street of the housing estate left partly unbuilt by Gropius.

On 16 January 1945, twenty-five houses of the housing estate were destroyed in an air raid. These were later replaced by structures that are largely similar in form. And yet, as if the residents wanted to counter the monotony of mass housing through distinct individualisation, the structural modifications, which had begun as early as the 1930s, were continued in the GDR by adding individual extensions or making alterations. Because of this, the aesthetic minimalism and the homogeneity have been lost. Only a few houses were renovated according to the original plans or give a more or less vague impression of their original appearance.

Today, the housing estate is protected under heritage preservation laws, and since 1994 has at its disposal a preservation and design statute which stipulates that any additional changes to the façade must be made based on the original design. Most houses, however, continue to be privately owned and, through their acquisition by the residents, attest in a different way to the success of the housing estate project. One type-I house from the first construction stage and one type-IV house are publicly owned and accessible to visitors.

The high-voltage line was already there when construction of the housing estate began and provided crucial reference points for the urban planning concept for the estate. The green area under the line (on the right) was part of these plans. The individual houses have been heavily modified.

The residence of the Anton family has largely been preserved in its original state. The family lived in it until 2001. It now belongs to the city of Dessau-Roßlau. The glass blocks at the entrance (right) were elaborately remoulded in the course of renovation.

The staired hallway leads straight to the eat-in kitchen, whose technical features, including a bathtub, were considered advanced in the 1920s. The house has xylolite screed floors and also terrazzo flooring in the kitchen (right). The kitchen is clearly divided into a cooking area and a scullery.

Upstairs, there were three bedrooms (left). One of them provided access to the roof terrace (large image), which was ideal for sunbathing. The roof terrace offers a good view of the long, narrow subsistence gardens.

In the attached stable was the so-called Metroclo, a composting toilet developed by the garden architect Leberecht Migge. Its contents were composted together with other waste and scraps and eventually reused as manure for the garden.

On Mittelring, two houses of the SieTö IV type were renovated for the Moses Mendelssohn Society. They give visitors an impression of the smallest of the realised house types in Dessau-Törten. The ribbon windows had been replaced with other formats and were reconstructed during renovation.

In the SieTö I house (right), the stairs were moved closer to the entrance in the second construction phase to create more space for the eat-in kitchen. SieTö II (left) is not fully cellared and its partial basement to the right of the entrance already announces the split level of SieTö IV.

SieTö II houses were also built in traditional brick construction (top left) to allow a direct comparison with concrete construction. The Konsum Building (right) stands in the centre of the housing estate and provided groceries for the residents. The pump station (bottom left) was repeatedly modified and repurposed.

STEEL HOUSE

GEORG MUCHE AND RICHARD PAULICK 1926/27

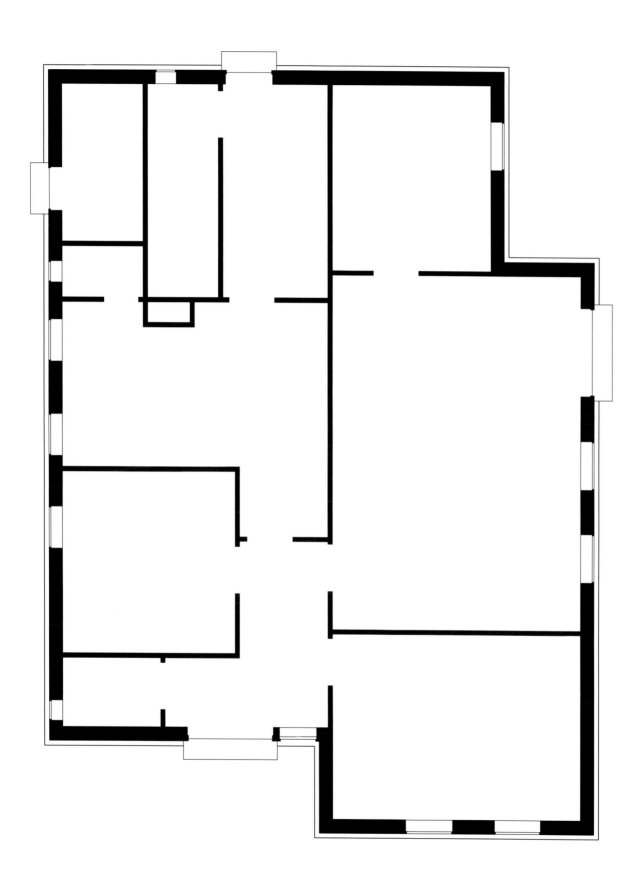

Ground floor

Between 1926 and 1927, a "metal modular house" designed by Georg Muche and Richard Paulick was built in cooperation with the Leipzig bank vault builder Carl Kästner AG on a site at the north edge of the Dessau-Törten Housing Estate and in the immediate vicinity of the Fieger House. Realised as an experimental building as part of the first construction phase of the housing estate, the so-called Steel House was intended to demonstrate the possibilities of industrial steel construction – which is why it was already possible to visit the construction site when the Bauhaus Building was inaugurated on 4 December 1926. Unlike most steel houses of the day, the Dessau version combined the innovative construction with a thoroughly modern design.

In Dessau, the painter and architect Georg Muche had been working with the then architecture student Richard Paulick, an associate in the private architecture office of Walter Gropius, on the development of industrially prefabricated, extendable houses with flexible floor plans. This research resulted in the single-storey, basement-less and detached experimental steel building which, with its 90 square metres of living area and similar layout, exceeded the terraced houses of the Dessau-Törten Housing Estate in terms of surface area. By using floor-to-ceiling doors in the lower part of the building and higher ceilings in the living and bedroom, the architects achieved a spaciousness and variety in terms of space which the neighbouring terraced houses of Walter Gropius lack.

The Steel House comprises two merged cubes of different height under a flat roof and is thus reminiscent of the Haus Am Horn, which Muche had realised in 1923 for the first Bauhaus exhibition in Weimar. The walls of his Dessau experimental building consist of a steel skeleton to which steel panels were attached on the outside and plastered cinder blocks on the inside. A course of Torfoleum, an insulating material used in many Dessau Bauhaus buildings, was inserted between those layers. This construction method allowed for prefabrication of the steel panels complete with openings for doors and windows, as well as the subsequent installation of the individual components by workers on-site.

The edges of the steel panels were protected with cover strips. These strips and the tall, narrow window sizes lend the building's exterior its characteristic vertical structuring. As a second window format, ancillary spaces such as toilet and pantry received bull's-eye windows, which let in light but prevent people from looking in. Grey, white and black make up the building's outside colour scheme.

One enters the house from the south-west. Passing through the entry hallway, one reaches to the right the bedroom and the living room, which has another, smaller room attached to it. To the left, one reaches the toilet and a second bedroom and, straight ahead, the dining kitchen, from which one has access to the bathroom and laundry room, a pantry and a box room. The storage room for the coal used to heat the building is accessible only from outside. This layout reduced access areas to a minimum.

The Dessau Steel House is one of the numerous attempts made at the time to use the industrial material steel for housing construction as well. However, it did not catch on, and so it is perhaps not surprising that the prototype by Muche and Paulick was criticised soon after its completion: it was said to be too hot inside in the summer and too cold in the winter. A longer-term tenant did not move in until 1932.

The Steel House was used for residential purposes up to the 1990s and underwent extensive renovation in 1992–93. Today, it belongs to the Bauhaus Dessau, which makes it accessible to the public through special exhibitions, events and guided tours.

The house consists of steel panels whose edges were protected by cover strips. These, together with the tall, narrow window sizes, lend the exterior of the building its characteristic vertical structuring. The taller section of the building accommodates the living room and a bedroom.

The entrance is on the south side, while
the living room with two large windows and
a ground-level door opens to the east.

A view from the hallway to the entrance in the south gives an idea of the effect created by the varying ceiling heights and the thin walls. Entering from the lower-ceilinged hallway made the living room appear all the brighter and more spacious.

FIEGER HOUSE

CARL FIEGER
1927

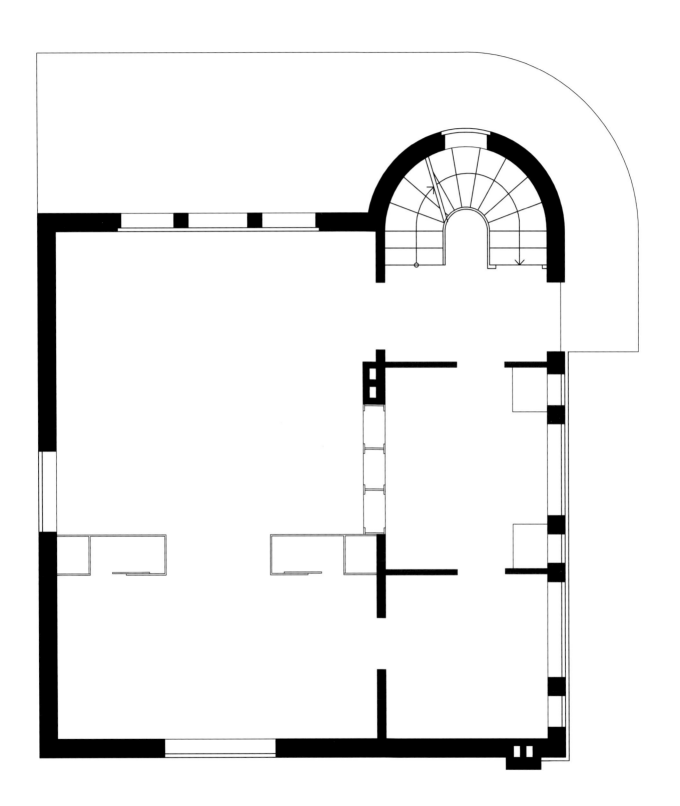

Ground floor

In 1927, Carl Fieger realised his private residence as one of the few buildings he built on his own account, with the Kornhaus Restaurant being the only other building he designed independently in Dessau. However, as a teacher at the Bauhaus and a long-time important associate in the architecture office of Walter Gropius, he was substantially involved in the designing of the Bauhaus Building, the Masters' Houses, the Employment Office and, not least, the Dessau-Törten Housing Estate. His own residence is indeed indebted to the functional formal vocabulary of Gropius's architecture office.

The site on which the Fieger House stands was previously one of the gravel pits for the first construction stage of the Dessau-Törten Housing Estate. This obviated the need to excavate the full cellar for the single-family home. With a floor area of 74 square metres, it is consistent with the "SieTö I-type" row houses. For his detached residence, Fieger drew on a design he had already published in 1926 in the magazine *Bauwelt*. For the site in Törten, Fieger reworked the design. With its highly rational and flexible interior configuration on a square plan, the two-storey Fieger House may be seen as the result of various studies by Fieger on the optimisation of floor plans and on small residential buildings.

Upon entering the house on the west-facing street side, a hallway led to the living space, which opened up towards the southeast, facing the terrace and garden in front of it. Immediately adjacent to it to the north was the bedroom, which during the day could also be used as a living area thanks to its large doorway and the kind of furnishings it featured. A door to the left in the hallway opened to the kitchen, which was connected to the dining area in the living room by a pass-through in the fitted cupboard. The bathroom was located in the north corner of the house, between the kitchen and the bedroom, and had doors opening to both.

A semicircular staircase led up to the second storey, whose L-shape framed an almost square roof terrace above the living room. This terrace protrudes from the square of the rest of the structure, thereby significantly contributing to the sculptural appearance of the small cubic building. From the upper stair landing, one door opened to the roof terrace and another to the study, which was followed by a children's room and, finally, a storeroom.

The Bauhäusler Hans Volger and Heinz Nösselt were involved in the construction of the Fieger House as interns. All interior furnishings were designed by Fieger and manufactured in the Bauhaus workshops. The façade was originally painted a striking lemon yellow and the window and door frames a cobalt blue.

Carl Fieger and his wife, Dora, spent only a few months in the house before leaving with Walter Gropius and his architecture office for Berlin in 1928 and subsequently letting the house. In 1945, the Fiegers returned to their Dessau home. In 1960, a few years after Carl Fieger's death, his widow eventualy sold the house. In subsequent years, an extension with a cellar was built. The house remains privately owned and is therefore not open to the public.

The Fieger House is privately owned and not open to the public. The garden is now overgrown with bushes and trees which, in addition to obstructing the exterior view, is not consistent with the austere, plain and functional gardens of most other Bauhaus buildings.

HOUSES WITH BALCONY ACCESS

BAUHAUS BUILDING DEPARTMENT UNDER THE DIRECTION OF HANNES MEYER 1930

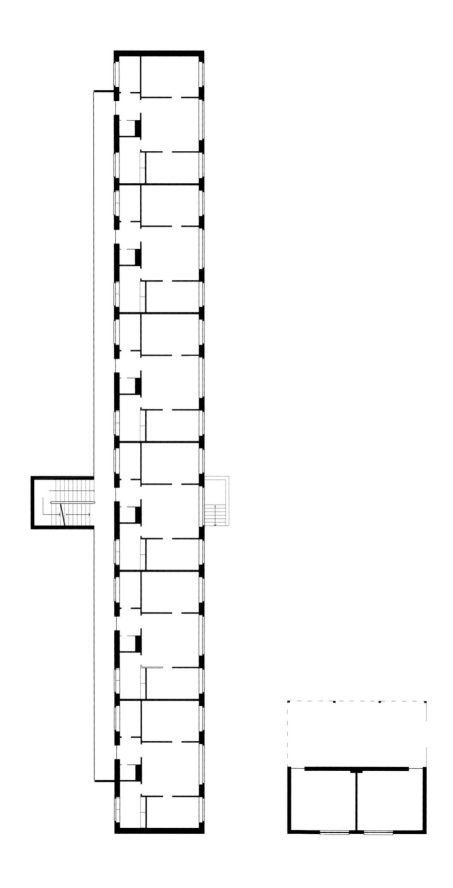

Ground floor

To the south of the three construction phases realised by Walter Gropius and his architecture office between 1926 and 1928, the Bauhaus Building Department headed by Hannes Meyer planned an expansion of the Dessau-Törten Housing Estate. The concerns of the second Bauhaus director are often summed up by the motto "The needs of the people instead of the need for luxury", yet in addition to greater emphasis on the social aspects of architecture, his interests included a scientific approach to all issues of architecture and town planning. The Houses with Balcony Access on Peterholzstrasse and Mittelbreite are, along with the row houses designed by Richard Paulick, the only buildings of the planned housing estate expansion to be realised in a modern architectural style. Together with the Trade Union School of the ADGB in Bernau, near Berlin, they testify more than any other work of the Bauhaus to the pedagogic and creative ambitions of the Dessau school during Meyer's tenure. In 2017, the Houses with Balcony Access were named a UNESCO World Heritage site, joining the Bauhaus Building and the Masters' Houses, which have been listed since 1996.

In 1927, when Walter Gropius appointed Hannes Meyer head of the Building Department to be established at the Bauhaus in Dessau – he would succeed Gropius as the second Bauhaus director in 1928 – Meyer's focus in terms of his pedagogic thinking was on connecting theory to construction practice. This is why the building contract of the Dessau Spar- und Baugenossenschaft (Savings and Building Cooperative) went to the Building Department of the Bauhaus as a collective and not, as it had been in Gropius's day, to the director's private architecture office, which would then allow students to become involved. Viewed as a collective by Meyer, the Building Department began to develop the town-planning concept for the expansion in 1928. Ludwig Hilberseimer, who was in charge of building theory from the spring of 1929 on, provided essential town-planning impulses. The development plan originally provided for ten houses with balcony access and 531 single-storey detached houses, as well as houses with balcony access on the west edge of the housing estate (realised by Richard Paulick as row houses) – a town layout that was supposed to be conducive to a social mix within the housing estate.

Five of the planned houses with balcony access were eventually realised by a student collective. The students worked on the design, construction management and billing and were paid for their work. To make the housing as inexpensive as possible, the floor plans and the construction were optimised from a scientific point of view. The living areas, meaning the bedrooms and sitting rooms, were located on the south side of the houses in order to benefit from natural light entering through large windows, while ancillary rooms such as kitchens and bathrooms were arranged to face north with smaller windows. Also located on the north side are the glazed stairwells and the access balconies. The classical vestibule was replaced by the access balconies and thus moved outdoors. Keeping the circulation largely open saved material as well as construction and heating costs. The structure was left unclad and the clear design of the red brick façade and the continuous reinforced concrete beams show the materiality and the way the building was constructed. The arrangement and size of the windows point to the functions of the spaces behind them.

The five three-storey apartment buildings have a total of more than ninety flats with a floor area of 48 square metres each. One enters the entrance hallway from the access balcony: to the right is the heater with the coal box, to the left the bathroom with toilet and enamelled bathtub. Straight ahead is the central living area, from which one can access both the parents' and the children's bedrooms. Each apartment building had a garden for the tenants and a communal garden area, a washhouse, a bleachery and a children's playground. The furnishings were partly provided by the Bauhaus workshops.

The functional Houses with Balcony Access continue to testify to the social aspiration and extraordinary quality of the scientifically based planning and clear-cut design of the Bauhaus under Meyer. Today, they continue to serve, largely unchanged, residential purposes, though the floor plans and the windows have been adapted to meet present-day requirements. One of the flats is leased by the Bauhaus Dessau Foundation and may be visited as part of a guided tour.

Facing north, the access balconies promote interaction among the residents. The original metal-frame windows were replaced with plastic-frame windows.

The extensively glazed staircases (left) were walled up in four of the five Houses with Balcony Access (centre). The smaller window openings now let in less light but are easier to clean. Each house also has its own washhouse in the gardens (right).

View from the parents' bedroom through the living room to the children's room. Each room has its own colour scheme. Radiators and pipes were accentuated rather than hidden.

Behind the front door on the right, this house still has the central heating system with coal box. In the narrow kitchen (right), built-in fitments create sufficient room for efficient work even in the smallest space. Under the back of the built-in cupboard in the children's room, there is still enough space for the end of a bed.

PAULICK ROW HOUSES

RICHARD PAULICK
1931

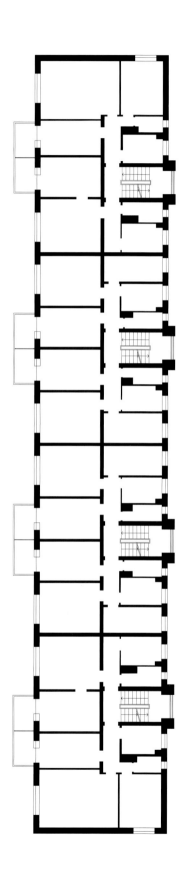

Upper floor

The row houses, also known as "DEWOG Houses", were built in 1931 on behalf of Deutsche Wohnungsfürsorge AG (DEWOG; German housing assistance). The architect Richard Paulick provided the plans and the work was carried out by Gemeinnützige Wohnungs- und Heimstätten GmbH Dresden (GEWOG; non-profit housing company). The Paulick Row Houses concluded the building activities of the Bauhaus or of architects closely associated with it in Dessau-Törten. The single-family homes with pitched roofs which were subsequently built as part of the expansion of the housing estate adhere to a different, more traditional understanding of architecture.

Paulick, who had been an associate in Gropius's architecture office from 1926 until 1929, realised the seven rows of four-storey houses as an independent architect, basing his designs on the town-planning concept the Building Department of the Bauhaus had developed for the expansion of the Dessau-Törten Housing Estate. However, instead of the row houses with their conventional stairwells, the original plans were for houses with balcony access like those that had been realised shortly before in the immediate vicinity under the direction of Hannes Meyer.

Along Heidestrasse, a street running north to south, the shorter sides of the rows of houses face the street, while four stairwells each on the north side provide access and the living areas face the sunny side. Each row of houses has thirty-two two- or three-room flats. Each flat has a balcony facing south, while ancillary rooms such as kitchen, bathroom and small room are on the side facing north. The horizontal window formats on the south side are, as befits their residential purpose, considerably larger than the vertical-format punch windows in the north façade, which is strictly subdivided by the four slightly protruding stairwells. The design of the stairwells with their generous glazing in steel sections is reminiscent of Meyer's Houses with Balcony Access. The solidly built row houses were rendered above the clinker brick base and had flat roofs.

While the construction method of the row houses was not innovative, their layout and design were in large part consistent with the ideas and convictions the Bauhaus had put into practice in the preceding years. As in previous years, the Junkers Steelworks, which had already played an important role in the decision to move the Bauhaus to Dessau, were enlisted for the installation of fixtures in the flats. Featuring central heating, hot and cold running water, a hip bath and flush lavatories, the furnishings of the row houses met the demands of the time.

By 1934, the Paulick Row Houses had already been significantly altered through the addition of pitched roofs with extended dormers in order to create space for fifty-six additional small flats. This modification may also be regarded as an ideological decision taken under National Socialist rule: the Nazis vilified the works of numerous Bauhäusler along with those of other modern artists and architects. If they could not be torn down, then the appearance of

the modern buildings had at least to be adapted to the new ideo-logical circumstances. The single-storey shops erected between the row houses along Heidestrasse survive to this day.

A renovation in the 1990s then changed the modernist build-ings beyond recognition: external insulation and new windows in plastic frames with three panes instead of four were installed and the previously delicate balcony railings were replaced by closed parapets. Inside, some details from the time of construction are still preserved. The houses are still occupied and therefore not open for viewing.

No longer recognisable today as modernist buildings, the so-called row houses received pitched roofs during the National Socialist period. In the 1990s, the façade was insulated, the balconies were renovated and the windows replaced. Only the basement windows still feature the original window divisions.

AUTHOR AND PHOTOGRAPHER BIOGRAPHIES

FLORIAN STROB was born near Osnabrück in 1985. He studied German literature and modern history in Bonn and at Oxford, earning his doctorate from the latter in 2013 with a literary studies dissertation. He subsequently studied architecture at the Technical University of Berlin. His research interests focus on the interfaces between literature and architecture. Since 2018, Strob has been a research associate at the Bauhaus Dessau Foundation, where, among other responsibilities, he has been developing the new curatorial programme for the Bauhaus Building and the Masters' Houses. He lives and works in Berlin and Dessau-Roßlau.

THOMAS MEYER was born in Delmenhorst, Lower Saxony, in 1967. He attended the University of the Arts in Bremen and completed his master class under Arno Fischer at the Ostkreuz School of Photography in Berlin. Meyer's photographs are characterised above all by a focused play of proximity and distance, which enables them them to elicit new and surprising aspects from the supposedly familiar. Meyer has been a member of the renowned OSTKREUZ agency since 2000. He lives and works in Berlin.

ACKNOWLEDGEMENTS

I would like to begin by thanking Caroline Jansky and Thomas Meyer. I thank Caroline for her superb organisational support in bringing this book project to fruition. She was always the first to read the texts, and her critical notes made a significant contribution to the successful completion of the work. Collaborating with Thomas has been a real pleasure. His unerring eye was often enlightening when viewing the buildings. This book would not have been conceivable without him and his enthusiasm.

A book such as this is, of course, always based on various publications by numerous researchers, whom I would expressly like to thank for their often decades-long research. Since a scholarly treatise was not planned and footnotes therefore had to be dropped, allow me to mention a few names here as representative of many others: Christine Engelmann and Christian Schädlich, Monika Markgraf, Robin Rehm, Andreas Schwarting and Wolfgang Thöner. Among the colleagues at the Bauhaus Dessau Foundation who were always ready to generously share their knowledge even in personal conversation, I gratefully acknowledge the assistance provided by Peter Bernhard, Regina Bittner, Torsten Blume, Werner Möller and Lutz Schöbe.

I also extend particular thanks to Monika Markgraf for reviewing the manuscript and making valuable suggestions regarding all aspects of the buildings' histories. Her book *Die Dessauer Bauhausbauten* (Bauhaus Taschenbuch 16) has in every respect been an important basis for our work.

Thanks are due to Hirmer Publishing for suggesting that we undertake this publication and for their excellent cooperation.

My warmest thanks also go to Mrs. Rauchfuss for agreeing to have photographs taken inside the Haus Hahn. Finally, I would like to thank Claudia Perren for her confidence in this project and concept.

Florian Strob

IMPRINT

This catalogue has been published in conjunction with the "100 Years of Bauhaus" anniversary.

Edited by
Bauhaus Dessau Foundation

Director: Claudia Perren
Gropiusallee 38
06846 Dessau-Roßlau

www.bauhaus-dessau.de

Author: Florian Strob
Photographer: Thomas Meyer
Editor: Caroline Jansky
Expert advice: Monika Markgraf
Project direction, Hirmer Verlag: Kerstin Ludolph
Translation from the German: Bram Opstelten
Copy-editing: Danko Szabó
Layout, typesetting and production: Sophie Friederich
Pre-press: Reproline Mediateam GmbH, Unterföhring
Printing and binding: Printer Trento S.r.l.
Paper: Gardamatt Art, 150 g
Typeface: Halyard

Printed in Italy

www.hirmerpublishers.com

978-3-7774-3202-1 (English edition)
978-3-7774-3199-4 (German edition)

Front cover: Walter Gropius, Bauhaus Building stairwell, 1925/26

Bibliographical data of the Deutsche Nationalbibliothek: The Deutsche Nationalbibliothek lists this publication in the Deutschen Nationalbibliografie; detailed bibliographic information is available on the Internet at http://www.dnb.de.

© 2019 Bauhaus Dessau Foundation, Hirmer Verlag GmbH, Munich, and the author

The Bauhaus Dessau Foundation is a non-profit foundation under public law. It is institutionally funded by:

Bauhaus
Dessau

#moderndenken

 jahre bauhaus

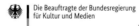 Die Beauftragte der Bundesregierung für Kultur und Medien

 SACHSEN-ANHALT

Hier macht das Bauhaus Schule.

Dessau ⌐ Roßlau

PHOTO CREDITS